fantastico!

GINO D'ACAMPO

fantastico!

Modern Italian Food

Photography by *Kate Whitaker*

KYLE BOOKS

To my grandfather who is no longer with us,
but his passion for food still lives in me!

Contents

Introduction

I grew up in the south of Italy, in Napoli, surrounded by a very large family, so it is no wonder that I became passionate about food. The food we ate was very traditional; simple recipes based on fresh and healthy fruit, vegetables, fish and meat. My grandfather always said that a good recipe doesn't need many ingredients, because if the ingredients are good quality and full of flavour, why do you have to cover up or change their taste? In the summer of 1987 when I was eleven, I walked into my grandfather's restaurant for the first time and that's when I decided that this was the career for me too.

That same summer I decided to go to catering college so that I could train to be a chef. Why? Simple. To me there is nothing more satisfying than seeing people enjoy a meal that you have created. That is the reason why I decided to write a book – so that everyone can enjoy the same experience. I wanted to write a book that would finally answer all the questions that people ask me about Italian cuisine – because, believe it or not, some of you are still making the same mistakes over and over again.

Enough… let me tell you what I think: there is no such thing as 'I can't cook'. There is a chef in each and everyone of us, but the problem is that you don't know it yet. Let me explain why. Cooking comes from the heart. If you feel down or upset, it will show in the taste of your dishes and, no matter how hard you try to follow my recipes, I guarantee you that it will be a disaster. My grandfather used to say to me that practice makes perfect; he was right, but I also say that practising for the wrong reasons will never be a success. My first rule of cooking therefore is: if you are not in a good mood, don't attempt to cook. Get a takeaway!

My second rule is cook alone. Don't try to cook with someone else, or in a group. Cooking is a personal experience, as I've just explained, and your personality will show in the food you prepare, so communal cooking will only confuse the dish. Cooking should be a selfish and relaxing experience; selfish because it is probably the only time that you should think about what YOU like and how to satisfy yourself, and relaxing because it is definitely the only time you shouldn't think about anything else, especially your problems – otherwise refer back to rule number 1.

Rule number 3 is don't try to make a 'healthier' version of a recipe; get your arse down the gym. This is self-explanatory.

The fourth rule: never cook onions and garlic together. I remember very clearly my first day at catering school. I was 14 years old and on my first attempt at making a simple tomato sauce, as I was frying my onions and garlic together, the headteacher came to me and said, 'remember Gino, the secret of a good dish is respecting the ingredients that you use'. Soon afterwards he taught me to understand the unique flavours that onions and garlic have and explained that these two great ingredients should never be mixed together. Today, none of my recipes have onions and garlic cooked together and I choose my flavours very carefully.

Rule number 5: put all your energy and concentration into the flavour of a dish and worry less about what a dish looks like. If you get the recipe right, it will look so appetising that you won't need to worry about its presentation.

Finally, and I can't say this often enough, spend less time on cooking a dish and more time on buying the right ingredients. How many times have you had to cook something for a long time with so many herbs and spices just to give an extra kick to the dish? Take a curry, for example. Some people say 'hoooo!, it's an explosion of flavours'. I say, tell me, what am I supposed to taste in a curry? The experience and the enjoyment of eating a good dish is by tasting, recognising and appreciating every single ingredient that you have put together. Next time you pick up a carrot, close your eyes, smell it, and then you will know what I mean.

I hope this book will prove to you that you don't need to spend a lot of time in the kitchen to enjoy a good Italian meal. It will also give you a good idea of the food you will find in Italy now. I have chosen some traditional recipes, exactly as my grandfather would have cooked them, some modern dishes, sometimes with a twist of my own, and a few that have been influenced by food that I love from other countries. None of the recipes are complicated or fussy – just get the ingredients right, buy a sharp knife and fantastico!

My book will tell you everything you need to know about Italian cooking – all my rules, tips and secrets – so by the time you have tried the recipes, you will understand my motto:

Minimum effort, maximum satisfaction!

First Aid for Food

1. If you want to make a good tomato salad but the tomatoes aren't as good as they could be, make sure that, after you have sliced them, you season them with salt and pepper, a good drizzle of extra virgin olive oil and a few fresh basil leaves. This will bring out their maximum flavour.

2. When you buy Mozzarella in a tub or bag filled with water from a supermarket, it is usually the commercially produced sort with not a lot of flavour. To get the best out of it, drain the Mozzarella, slice it on a serving plate, sprinkle over some salt and drizzle with good extra virgin olive oil.

3. If you have to use strawberries out of season, to get the best flavour, marinate them in Amaretto liqueur, or alternatively, add some caster sugar and freshly squeezed lemon juice. Leave to marinate for at least 20 minutes.

4. If your fruit is unripe but you still want to make a tasty fresh fruit salad, place your chopped or sliced fruit in a large bowl and dress it with Limoncello liqueur and icing sugar. Leave to marinate for at least 30 minutes.

5. If you have salad leaves that are reaching their sell-by date and are starting to wilt, remember you can always use them for cooking as you would use rocket leaves.

6. If your apples are too ripe, use them to make a fantastic apple sauce like the one used for the Maiale al Pepe e Sciroppo on page 101.

7. If your recipe only requires egg yolks, please do not throw away the whites. You can use them to make a great meringue like the one on page 149 (Cesto di Frutta).

8. If your avocados are too ripe or have gone dark in the middle, blitz them with some balsamic vinegar, salt and olive oil until smooth, to make an exquisite dipping sauce for your favourite crisps or pitta bread.

9. If you have bought too many lemons and they are past their best, squeeze the juice into an ice-cube tray. Once they have hardened, pop them out, place them in a plastic food bag and keep in the freezer. Great to add to a soft drink or plain water instead of an ice cube.

10. If your bread is becoming stale, do not throw it away. Cut into chunks, place on a baking tray and cook in a preheated oven set to 180°C/350°F/gas mark 4 for about 20 minutes. Once golden and brown, remove from the oven and allow to cool. Blitz in a food processor to make toasted breadcrumbs. Store in a plastic food bag in your cupboard for up to three months. Excellent for making escalope or fried fish.

In Italy brunch doesn't exist. We start the morning with a croissant and a cappuccino and we starve ourselves until lunchtime, but let me tell you, an Italian lunch is not a regular lunch; it is a two-hour feast with a four-course meal followed by a siesta. Since I've been living here (nearly 13 years), my way of life has changed and the hours in my day are filled differently. I never get the chance to have a long meal followed by a siesta anymore.

So mid-morning is probably my worst dilemma. It's 11am and I'm hungry. It's definitely too early for a big lunch, so I'm going to choose something lighter and probably skip lunch – what do I choose?

Cooking tips – only one...

1. Make sure you have some kind of small snack lying around for about 4pm – you will be hungry again before your dinner!

Date and Raisin Pancakes with Caramel Sauce

PANCAKES ALLA FRUTTA

Serves 4

100g pitted dates, chopped

90g raisins

1 teaspoon bicarbonate of soda

250g self-raising flour

90g soft brown sugar

250g sour cream

3 medium eggs, separated

Melted butter, for greasing

Pineapple, mango, papaya, banana, or a seasonal selection of fresh fruit of your choice

FOR THE SAUCE

250ml single cream

180g soft brown sugar

200g salted butter

This is my little sister Marcella's favourite recipe. Obviously, it's not very Italian, but it's still good enough to be in my book. I absolutely love the texture and the fruits that I have chosen. Make sure that when you prepare the pancakes, you stack them one on top of each other, creating a tower effect, and completely cover them with the warm caramel sauce. Also great for dessert.

Put the dates and raisins in a small saucepan with 250ml of water and bring to the boil. Remove from the heat, stir in the bicarbonate of soda and set aside to cool. Place in a food-processor and blitz until smooth.

Sift the flour into a large bowl and use a wooden spoon to mix in the sugar and the raisin mixture.

Beat together the sour cream and egg yolks in a separate bowl and pour into the flour mixture. Stir until you have a smooth batter and set aside for 20 minutes.

Whisk the egg whites in a large, spotlessly clean bowl until soft peaks form and fold into the batter.

Heat a medium frying pan over a medium heat and lightly brush with melted butter.

Pour about 1 ladleful of batter into the pan and cook for 3 minutes until bubbles form on the surface. Turn over and cook the other side for 2 minutes. Transfer to a warm plate and cover with a tea-towel while you make up the rest of the pancakes.

To prepare the caramel sauce, place all the ingredients in a medium saucepan over a medium heat and allow to dissolve. Gently simmer for 4–5 minutes, stirring occasionally.

Serve the sauce over the warm pancakes with some fresh fruit.

Eggs with Mediterranean Vegetables in Tomato Sauce

Serves 4

3 tablespoons olive oil

1 medium onion, sliced

3 medium courgettes, roughly chopped

1 large yellow pepper, roughly chopped

400g tinned chopped tomatoes

5 fresh basil leaves

50g pitted Kalamata olives

4 medium eggs

70g freshly grated Cheddar cheese

Salt and pepper

This is a fantastic way to cook your eggs. The combination of the ingredients is just unbelievable. You can prepare the sauce well ahead and when you are ready, reheat it and break in the eggs as the recipe explains. Ensure you serve plenty of bread with this dish to soak up the delicious sauce.

Heat the olive oil in a large frying pan and fry the onion, courgettes and pepper until soft and browned, stirring occasionally. Season with salt and pepper, add in the tomatoes, basil and olives. Cook, uncovered, over a medium heat for about 10 minutes or until the water from the tomatoes is well reduced.

Meanwhile, preheat the grill. Make four slight hollows in the tomato mixture and very gently break one egg into each. Sprinkle over the cheese and cook under the grill for about 10 minutes or until the eggs are set as you like them.

Serve immediately with warm crusty bread.

The Ultimate Egg-fried Bread with Melted Mozzarella

MOZZARELLA IN CARROZZA

Serves 2

3 medium eggs

3 tablespoons freshly grated Parmesan cheese

2 cow's milk Mozzarella balls, drained and sliced

4 slices of country-style nut bread, about 2cm thick

2 tablespoons pesto sauce

4 slices of cooked ham

10 tablespoons olive oil

Salt and pepper

Every time my father visits, he always ensures that I have all these ingredients. Since I can remember, this has always been his favourite dish. Make sure you use a cow's Mozzarella not buffalo Mozzarella, because the latter contains too much milk.

Beat the eggs and Parmesan together in a large bowl and season.

Divide the Mozzarella slices between two slices of bread, spread with pesto and top with two slices of ham, then place the remaining bread on top.

Heat the oil in a large frying pan. Dip the sandwiches into the egg mixture, then lower them into the hot oil and cook over a medium heat for about 2 minutes on each side to allow the Mozzarella to melt and the outside to become crisp. When cooked, transfer to kitchen paper to allow any excess oil to drain and rest for 2 minutes. Cut the sandwiches in half and serve with some of your favourite crisps.

Scrambled Eggs with Pancetta, Peas and Asparagus

UOVA STRAPAZZATE

Serves 2

150g asparagus spears, trimmed

2 tablespoons olive oil

150g pancetta, finely chopped

100g frozen peas, thawed

5 medium eggs

50ml full-fat milk

50g salted butter

1 small ciabatta loaf, sliced

Salt and pepper

Cook the asparagus in a small pan of boiling salted water for no longer than 4 minutes. Drain and rinse gently under cold water to prevent the asparagus from discolouring. Pat dry on kitchen paper, then roughly chop the stalks and reserve the tips.

Heat the olive oil in a small pan and fry the pancetta and peas for about 10 minutes or until the pancetta is golden and crisp.

Whisk the eggs with the milk in a large bowl and season.

Melt the butter in a medium frying pan, add the egg mixture and stir with a wooden spoon over a medium heat until it starts to set. Tip in the pancetta, peas and the asparagus stalks and stir until the eggs are lightly set.

Serve the eggs immediately topped with the asparagus tips and accompanied with toasted ciabatta bread.

The Ultimate Toasted Ciabatta with Italian Hummus and Grilled Sausages

Serves 2

4 Italian sausages

1 large ciabatta loaf

A few salad leaves of your choice

FOR THE HUMMUS

400g tinned chickpeas, drained and rinsed

Juice of 1 lemon

1 garlic clove

50ml light tahini paste

2 tablespoons extra virgin olive oil, plus extra for drizzling

50g pitted Kalamata olives

Salt and pepper

Since I left catering college, I've been everywhere in the Mediterranean to experience different cuisines, and after Italian food (of course), I think that Greek is probably my favourite. During the weekend, I often find myself in need of a hearty snack and this panino is always top of my list. The combination of crusty ciabatta bread, Italian sausages and hummus is absolutely divine.

With a sharp knife, cut the sausages lengthways, but without completely splitting into two halves, and cook on a hot griddle pan over a medium heat.

In the meantime, make the hummus. Put the chickpeas in a food-processor with the lemon juice, garlic, tahini paste, extra virgin olive oil and olives, blitz to a smooth paste. Once ready, season with salt and pepper.

With a serrated knife, slice the ciabatta lengthways, drizzle with some olive oil and grill with the sausages until it is crisp on both sides.

Once the sausages and the bread are ready, spread some of the Italian hummus on each side of the toasted bread, add the sausages, place some salad on top and enjoy immediately.

Neapolitan-style Pizza Topped with Anchovies

PIZZA ALLA NAPOLETANA

Makes 2 pizzas

Pinch of salt

1 teaspoon dried yeast

140ml warm water

180g strong plain flour, plus extra for dusting

1 tablespoon extra virgin olive oil, plus extra for greasing

FOR THE TOPPING

400g tinned chopped tomatoes

1 teaspoon dried oregano

10 anchovy fillets in oil

2 garlic cloves, finely sliced

4 tablespoons extra virgin olive oil

Salt and pepper

Napoli is a city well known for three things: 1. Vesuvius, 2. Gino D'Acampo and 3. Pizza. I could have written a whole book about pizzas, but I thought that I would show you the oldest pizza recipe known, which is actually the base for all other pizzas. I could eat pizza every day and I hope that everybody will try this recipe and enjoy making it. This is a great recipe to get children involved in cooking and there are no limits (except for pineapple!) for topping choices. Please make sure that the oven is preheated before you cook the pizza and that you place the topping on the pizza dough just before the pizza is ready to go in the oven.

To prepare the dough, mix the salt and yeast together in a jug with the water. Sift the flour into a large bowl, make a well in the centre and add the water mixture, along with the olive oil. Use a wooden spoon to mix everything well to create a wet dough.

Turn out the dough onto a clean well-floured surface and work it with your hands for about 5 minutes or until smooth and elastic. Place in a bowl and cover with a tea-towel. Leave in a warm place to rest for at least 45 minutes until the dough nearly doubles in size.

Meanwhile, preheat the oven to 220°C/425°F/gas mark 7.

Once rested, turn out the dough onto a floured surface, and divide it into two. Use your hands to push each out from the centre, creating two round discs about 25cm in diameter. Place the pizza bases on two oiled baking trays.

Spread the tomatoes on top of the pizza dough using a tablespoon and season with salt and pepper. Add a couple of pinches of oregano, the anchovies and garlic and drizzle with extra virgin olive oil. Cook in the middle of the oven for about 20 minutes or until golden and brown. Serve immediately.

Italian-style Cornish Pasty

CALZONE DI CARNE

Serves 4

250g plain flour

Pinch of salt

70g salted butter, cut into small dice

70g lard, cut into small dice

1 medium egg, beaten

FOR THE FILLING

250g beef steak, cut into small dice

1 medium swede, peeled and diced

1 onion, finely chopped

3 large potatoes, peeled and diced

150g smoked pancetta, diced

1 teaspoon finely chopped rosemary

Salt and pepper

To tell you the truth, I am such a big fan of the Cornish pasty that I had to create an Italian version of this dish. I can eat it hot, warm or cold and would always be satisfied by the flavours. Make sure you rest the dough for at least half an hour before you roll it out so that it relaxes, making it easier to work with.

Sift the flour into a large bowl with the salt. Use your fingers to rub in the butter and the lard and knead the dough to a firm consistency. Leave to rest for 30 minutes.

Preheat the oven to 200°C/400°F/gas mark 6.

Mix together the filling ingredients in a large bowl and season with salt and pepper. Divide the pastry into four balls and roll out into discs about 5mm thick. Share out the filling equally and pile in the middle of the discs. Dampen the edges of the pastry with water. Bring together the edges to enclose the filling. Pinch to seal and turn over the edges to make a rope-like effect.

Use the tip of a sharp knife to make a small slit on top of each calzone to let the steam out. Brush the top with beaten egg and place the calzone on an oiled baking tray.

Bake in the oven for 25 minutes, then reduce the heat to 180°C/350°F/gas mark 4 and cook for a further 25 minutes.

Serve immediately with your favourite salad.

Spicy Spaghetti Cake

FRITTATA DI SPAGHETTI

Serves 4

400g spaghetti

7 tablespoons olive oil

1 medium onion, finely chopped

1 teaspoon dry chilli flakes

2 medium courgettes, finely chopped

100g salame, finely sliced and chopped

5 medium eggs

200g freshly grated Pecorino cheese

4 tablespoons finely chopped parsley

Salt

If you like spaghetti, eggs and salame, you must try this recipe! The flavours are unbelievable and if you leave out the chilli, it is also a very child-friendly recipe. I've been eating this pasta dish since I can remember and I have to cook it for myself at least once a month to remind me of my home in Napoli. If you don't have spaghetti you can use tagliatelle or linguine and any hard cheese will do. Great to prepare the night before as it can be eaten cold for lunch the next day.

Cook the spaghetti in a large saucepan of boiling salted water until al dente. Drain and rinse under cold water to stop the pasta cooking. Drain again.

Heat 4 tablespoons of the olive oil in a large frying pan and fry the onion, chillies, courgettes and salame on a medium heat for 10 minutes until golden and soft. Season with salt and allow to cool.

Beat together the eggs, Pecorino and parsley in a large bowl. Add in the cooked onion mixture and the spaghetti. Mix well.

Heat the remaining olive oil in the same pan used to cook the onions. Add the spaghetti mixture and cook on a medium heat for 8 minutes on each side. You can finish off cooking the top side by placing the frying pan under a hot grill. Make sure that the spaghetti cake is a fantastic golden brown colour all over with a crispy texture.

Spinach and Gorgonzola Puffs

FAGOTTINI DI SPINACI

Serves 4

30g salted butter

½ onion, finely chopped

130g spinach leaves, washed

Whole nutmeg, for grating

100g Gorgonzola cheese

Ready-to-roll puff pastry
(2 x 25cm squares)

40g pistachio nuts, finely
chopped

1 medium egg, beaten

Olive oil, for greasing

FOR THE SALAD

250g rocket leaves

4 tablespoons extra virgin olive oil

2 tablespoons good-quality
balsamic vinegar

Salt and pepper

Often when I have friends coming round to my house and I want to prepare a lot of nibbles for them, I choose this recipe because it is so simple and I can prepare it before they arrive. My tip would be not to bother making puff pastry because the ready-made versions are perfectly fine. You can be very adventurous with this recipe; add Neopolitan salame, salame Milano or spicy chorizo, replace spinach with rocket leaves, or leave out any ingredients that you particularly don't like. For best results, serve them hot with a cold beer.

Melt the butter in a medium saucepan and gently fry the onion for 3 minutes or until softened. Add the spinach with plenty of grated nutmeg and cook for 5 minutes, stirring occasionally until the spinach is soft and the excess juice has evaporated. Season with salt and pepper, remove from the heat and leave to cool.

Preheat the oven to 200°C/400°F/gas mark 6. Cut each pastry square in half diagonally. Divide the spinach into four portions and place on one half of each pastry triangle. Top with Gorgonzola and sprinkle with pistachio nuts. Dampen the edges of the pastry with a little water, then fold over the pastry and press the edges to seal well. Brush with beaten egg to glaze.

Place the parcels on an oiled baking tray and cook in the oven for about 15 minutes or until golden brown and puffy.

Meanwhile, place the rocket leaves in a large bowl and dress with the olive oil and balsamic vinegar. Season with salt and pepper, mix well and serve with the puffs.

I love antipasti — this is the part of the meal that wakes up your taste buds. You will never go to an Italian house for dinner and not have some kind of antipasti, whether hot or cold or even both. Italians feel that this is probably the most important part of the meal. If you are serving aperitivi (drinks), offer them about 20 minutes before the antipasti, and make sure that they are good quality, so that you raise your guests' expectations of dinner.

You can have many different choices or just stick to one in particular, but the most important thing is to match it correctly to first your main dish and then your dessert.

Cooking tips

1. Try not to make anything too heavy — remember it's just a taste before your main meal arrives
2. Don't choose any fishy antipasti if your main meal is meat, otherwise you will ruin your palate
3. Don't serve too much antipasti which will fill up your guests too soon
4. If you have many people dining, choose easy antipasti, but impress them with good aperitivi
5. Make sure the aperitivi are always served cold
6. If you don't fancy making a main course, you can always make a meal based on antipasti
7. Never serve bread with olive oil — nobody does this in Italy

ADAMO

Any great dinner party should start with great aperitivi and this is definitely one of them. Make sure it is always served cold and prepare it at least five minutes before serving.

Serves 4

120ml freshly squeezed lemon juice

40ml sugar syrup (add 1½ tablespoons caster sugar to a pan with 100ml water and reduce to make 40ml)

240ml white rum

200g crushed ice cubes

Place the ingredients in a cocktail shaker. Shake for about 1 minute and serve immediately in tall glasses.

EVA

I think the title says it all – untrustworthy if you abuse it but delicious if you respect it. You can substitute the Prosecco for a good-quality Champagne and make sure that you serve Eva in a martini glass.

Serves 4

320ml freshly squeezed mandarin juice

480ml cold Prosecco

Divide the mandarin juice between four glasses. Top up with cold Prosecco and serve immediately in Martini glasses.

LUCIANO

I wanted to dedicate these two drinks to my two boys and the reasons are very simple: they are both sweet and beautiful, but at the same time they can be feisty and hazardous.

Serves 4

280g green apple nectar (available in supermarkets, but choose the thick nectar, not the juice)

40ml sugar syrup (add 1½ tablespoons caster sugar to a pan with 100ml water and reduce to make 40ml)

480ml Champagne

Mix the apple nectar and sugar syrup together and divide between four tall narrow glasses. Top up with cold Champagne and serve immediately.

ROCCO

Serves 4

120ml good-quality gin

120ml Cointreau

30ml freshly squeezed lime juice

160g fresh pineapple, cut into small cubes

80g small strawberries (ideally wild)

200g crushed ice cubes

Place all the ingredients in a cocktail shaker. Shake for about 30 seconds, and pour immediately in Martini glasses.

Mushrooms Stuffed with Gorgonzola and Honey

Serves 4

16 large button mushrooms

100g runny honey

400g Gorgonzola cheese (it must be at room temperature)

6 tablespoons extra virgin olive oil

1 ciabatta loaf, sliced

2 garlic cloves, cut in half

Salt and pepper

The combination of the strong cheese and the sweetness of the honey has always appealed to me. Try not to have fish after this recipe as I feel that its flavour is too powerful for fish.

Preheat the oven to 180°C/350°F/gas mark 4. Carefully remove the stalk from each mushroom to create a cavity ready to be stuffed. Discard the stalks. Rub a little honey on the inside of the mushrooms with the tip of your finger, then stuff each one with 1–2 teaspoons of Gorgonzola.

Place the mushrooms on a baking tray, season and drizzle with extra virgin olive oil. Cook in the oven for about 10 minutes.

Meanwhile, toast the bread on a hot griddle pan for about 3 minutes on each side or until dark brown and crusty, then rub the cut side of the garlic over the slices. Arrange the stuffed mushrooms on a large serving plate surrounded by the garlic bread and serve with cold beer.

Toasted Ciabatta Topped with Tomatoes and Basil

BRUSCHETTA CLASSICA

Serves 4

1 ciabatta loaf

4 tablespoons olive oil

400g small plum tomatoes

10 fresh basil leaves, sliced

6 tablespoons extra virgin olive oil, plus extra to serve

2 garlic cloves

This reminds me of my childhood when I went camping with my parents. My mother often served bruschetta for lunch. The secret is to add the topping at the last minute.

Cut the loaf into 8 slices, each 2cm thick, brush both sides with olive oil and toast on a hot griddle pan for about 3 minutes on each side or until dark brown and crusty. Leave to cool slightly.

Meanwhile, quarter the tomatoes and place in a bowl. Add the basil, extra virgin olive oil and season. Mix well and set aside, covered and at room temperature, for 5 minutes.

Lightly rub the garlic over the bread. Place 2–3 tablespoons of the tomato mixture on top of each slice and arrange the bruschette on a large serving plate. Drizzle with extra virgin olive oil, and enjoy.

Baked Aubergine with Mozzarella and Tomato Sauce

MELANZANE ALLA PARMIGIANA

Serves 4

6 large aubergines

Sea salt

10 tablespoons olive oil

200g plain flour

4 medium eggs, beaten and seasoned

3 Mozzarella balls, drained and sliced

300g freshly grated Parmesan cheese

20 fresh basil leaves

Sea salt and pepper

FOR THE TOMATO SAUCE

5 tablespoons olive oil

1 medium onion, finely chopped

2 sticks celery, finely chopped

1 large carrot, finely chopped

4 x 400g tinned chopped tomatoes

Salt and pepper

Sicily is a region in Italy that is famous for: 1. The Godfather, 2. The Mafia and 3. Melanzane alla Parmigiana. I remember when I was at catering college that one of the dishes I was really excited about learning to make was this one. Believe you me when I say that this is the ultimate Italian recipe. This dish is great eaten hot, warm or even cold.

To prepare the sauce, heat the olive oil in a large saucepan and gently fry the onion, celery and carrot until soft. Add the chopped tomatoes, season with salt and pepper and cook, uncovered, over a medium heat for about 10 minutes. Remove from the heat and leave to cool.

Meanwhile, cut the aubergines lengthways into slices about ½cm thick. Place in a sieve, sprinkle with sea salt and leave over the sink for about 1 hour to allow the excess water to drain from the aubergine. Place the slices on kitchen paper and pat dry.

Heat the oil in a large frying pan. Dust the aubergine slices first in flour, then dip in the eggs, and fry them in the hot oil until golden on both sides (you may need to work in batches). Transfer the slices to kitchen paper to drain off any excess oil.

Preheat the oven to 180°C/350°F/gas mark 4. Place a layer of aubergines in the base of a large ovenproof dish (about 40 x 20cm and 7cm deep). Spread about a fifth of the tomato sauce, then place some Mozzarella slices over the sauce. Sprinkle over a handful of Parmesan and some of the basil leaves. Repeat the process three times. Finally, spread the remaining tomato sauce on top and sprinkle with the remaining Parmesan. Cover with kitchen foil and bake in the oven for 20 minutes. Remove the foil and continue to bake for a further 30 minutes.

Remove from the oven and leave to rest for about 10 minutes before serving generous portions.

Deep-fried Taleggio with Strawberry Sauce

Serves 4

4 thick slices of Taleggio cheese
(each weighing about 100g)

100g plain flour

2 medium eggs, beaten

200g toasted breadcrumbs

1 litre vegetable oil, for frying

FOR THE STRAWBERRY SAUCE

4 tablespoons water

3 tablespoons balsamic vinegar

300g fresh strawberries, finely
chopped

Salt and pepper

Like most people, I am a big fan of all deep-fried food, but one of my favourites has to be deep-fried cheese. There is nothing better than the combination of crisp coating with melting cheese oozing inside, especially when it's served with a cool fruity sauce. You can substitute Taleggio for Brie, and if strawberries are out of season, you can use any other berries of your choice.

To prepare the sauce, reduce the water and balsamic vinegar in a saucepan by half, add the strawberries and gently cook for 3 minutes. Remove from the heat and leave to cool.

Meanwhile, dust each slice of Taleggio first in the flour, then dip in the eggs, and finally coat in breadcrumbs. Place the prepared cheese on a plate and leave to rest in the fridge for about 2 hours before cooking.

When you are ready to cook, heat the oil in a large, high-sided pan. Coat the Taleggio once again in the breadcrumbs. Carefully lower the slices into the hot oil and cook for about 3 minutes until they turn a golden colour. Transfer to a plate covered with kitchen paper to drain off any excess oil.

To serve, place 2–3 tablespoons of strawberry sauce in the centre of four plates and place a slice of Taleggio on top. Serve immediately to ensure that the cheese oozes out as soon as you break into the golden crust.

Courgettes with Truffle and Mint Dressing

ZUCCHINE E TARTUFO

Serves 4

4 medium courgettes

16 thin slices of white or black truffle

FOR THE DRESSING

6 tablespoons extra virgin olive oil

3 tablespoons good-quality balsamic vinegar

1 garlic clove, finely sliced

3 tablespoons finely sliced fresh mint leaves

Salt and pepper

This recipe sums up what this book is all about – minimum effort, maximum satisfaction! If you cannot find fresh truffles you can always use truffles preserved in jars or even truffle-flavoured olive oil.

To make the dressing, whisk together the olive oil, vinegar, garlic and mint in a large bowl and season with salt and pepper.

Thinly slice the courgettes lengthways using a swivel-blade potato peeler. Place the slices in the bowl with the dressing, season with more salt and pepper, mix well and leave to marinate for about 10 minutes.

To serve, pile the courgettes in the centre of four plates and top each serving with four slices of truffle. Serve with some warm crusty bread to mop up the dressing.

Figs and Soft Cheese Rolled in Parma Ham

Serves 4

6 large plum tomatoes

Extra virgin olive oil

6 large very ripe figs

200g soft cheese

5 tablespoons finely chopped fresh chives

12 slices Parma ham

4 tablespoons runny honey

Salt and pepper

This is a gorgeous antipasto that needs very little effort to prepare, yet looks and tastes fantastic. It was one of the first recipes I wrote as a chef, because I thought that the saltiness of the ham would go beautifully with the sweetness of the figs. The key to this dish is to prepare it just before you want to serve, otherwise the ham will go soggy. If you can't find fresh figs, use dark plums or mangoes instead. A typical Italian antipasto, these figs will go well with Bruschetta Classica or the Mushrooms Stuffed with Gorgonzola and Honey (both on page 29) — a contrast of hot and cold.

Preheat the grill. Cut the tomatoes in half and place on a baking tray, skin-side down. Season with salt and pepper, drizzle with extra virgin olive oil and grill for about 10 minutes until softened. Leave to cool.

Meanwhile, cut the figs in half, discarding the skin.

Mix the soft cheese with the chives and 1 tablespoon of extra virgin olive oil. Season with salt and pepper.

Lay a slice of ham lengthways on a chopping board. Place a fig half on one end. Drop a teaspoon of the soft cheese mixture on top of the fig, then place a tomato half on top of the cheese. Carefully roll up the ham to enclose the fig, cheese and tomato. Repeat with the remaining ingredients to make 12 parcels.

To serve, allow three parcels per portion. Drizzle with extra virgin olive oil and honey and enjoy with some toasted bread soldiers.

Deep-fried Polenta Sandwiches Stuffed with Salame Milano and Cheddar

BIGNÈ DI POLENTA ALLA MILANESE

Serves 4

400g polenta (use quick-cook polenta)

5 tablespoons finely chopped flat-leaf parsley

2 tablespoons plain flour, plus extra for dusting

16 slices Cheddar cheese

8 slices salame Milano

2 medium eggs

About ½ glass full-fat milk

1 litre vegetable oil, for frying

4 handfuls mixed salad leaves

4 tablespoons extra virgin olive oil

Juice of 1 lemon

Salt and pepper

If you travel anywhere in Italy north of Roma, you will find recipes using polenta. This recipe comes from Milano, but I've added an English twist. If you have not yet tried polenta, this is the best recipe to taste, because it's just full of flavour. My suggestion would be to always eat it hot or warm, because when cold, polenta tends to harden and become heavier in texture and taste. You can prepare large batches and warm them up before your guests arrive (great for parties). Make a batch without the salame for veggies.

Cook the polenta in boiling salted water according to the instructions on the packet until it thickens. Season with salt and pepper, add the parsley and stir well. Pour into a 15 x 11cm tray and level the top, ensuring that the polenta is about 1cm thick. Leave to cool until firm.

Once the polenta is cold and firm, use a drinking glass to cut out 16 discs about 7cm in diameter. Transfer them to a well-floured chopping board.

Place a slice of cheese on 8 discs, then a slice of salame and top with another slice of cheese. Cover with the remaining polenta discs to create small round sandwiches.

Beat the eggs in a large bowl with the flour, a couple of pinches of salt and pepper, then add enough milk to make a smooth batter.

Heat the oil in a large saucepan. Dip the polenta sandwiches into the batter and fry until golden and brown – work in batches, no more than four sandwiches at time. Once cooked, transfer the sandwiches to kitchen paper to allow the excess oil to drain. Serve immediately on a bed of fresh salad leaves dressed with extra virgin olive oil and freshly squeezed lemon juice.

Avocado with Saffron Crab

AVOCADO CON GRANCHIO

Serves 4

2 tablespoons olive oil

1 small onion, finely chopped

2 pinches of saffron stems

4 tablespoons ready-made mayonnaise

2 tablespoons tomato paste

Zest and juice of ½ unwaxed lemon

2 tablespoons finely chopped fresh chives

250g white crab meat, flaked

2 ripe avocados

Paprika, to garnish

Salt and pepper

Before I came to this country, I didn't have a clue what an avocado was – unfortunately in the south of Italy it is not part of our diet. Well, let me tell you, I am now converted and therefore I had to create a recipe using this fantastico fruit. Ensure that you buy ripe avocados and that they always come with a little stalk attached, because if not you might find that they are rotten on the inside.

Heat the olive oil in a small frying pan and gently fry the onion with the saffron for about 5 minutes or until soft. Remove from the heat and leave to cool.

Mix the mayonnaise with the tomato paste and the lemon zest and juice. Add in the chives and season with salt and pepper. Fold in the crabmeat with the onion and mix well.

Halve the avocados lengthways and gently remove the stones. Spoon the crab filling into the centres, sprinkle with paprika and serve.

Sardines Coated in Black Pepper with Italian Salsa

SARDINE AL PEPE NERO

Serves 4

300ml olive oil

2 garlic cloves, finely sliced

6 large plum tomatoes, chopped, seeds and skin included

100g pitted black olives, sliced

5 tablespoons chopped fresh basil

10 tablespoons toasted fine breadcrumbs

7 tablespoons black peppercorns, crushed

16 fresh sardines, gutted, heads and spines removed

200g plain flour

3 medium eggs, beaten and seasoned

100ml extra virgin olive oil

Salt and pepper

In Napoli, we eat a lot of sardines, especially cooked on the barbecue. The reason why I created this recipe is because sardines can be a very 'fishy' fish, but the black pepper coating balances this flavour perfectly. Always use fresh sardines and once cooked, do not reheat them. Absolutely fantastico eaten cold the next day for breakfast.

Heat 5 tablespoons of the olive oil in a large frying pan and fry the garlic until golden. Add the tomatoes and olives, season with salt and pepper and leave to cook over a medium heat for about 5 minutes. Add the chopped basil, then remove the salsa from the heat and leave to cool.

Meanwhile, mix the breadcrumbs and black pepper together on a plate.

Wash the sardines under cold running water and dry with kitchen paper. Dust each sardine first in the flour, dip into the eggs, then coat in the breadcrumbs and pepper.

Heat the remaining oil in a large frying pan and fry the sardines for about 2 minutes on each side – work in batches, no more than six sardines at a time. Once they look brown and crunchy, transfer to kitchen paper to allow any excess oil to drain.

Arrange four sardines on the plates with 2–3 tablespoons of the salsa. Drizzle with extra virgin olive oil and serve immediately.

Tuna and Sun-dried Tomato Fishcakes

Serves 4

250g potatoes, peeled

2 slices white bread, soaked in water and squeezed

2 medium eggs

2 x 200g tinned tuna chunks in oil, drained

100g sun-dried tomatoes in oil, drained and chopped

1 garlic clove, finely chopped

4 tablespoons chopped fresh flat-leaf parsley

Zest of 1 lemon, preferably unwaxed, and juice of half

150g toasted fine breadcrumbs

300g French green beans

50g sesame seeds

1 tablespoon extra virgin olive oil

Salt and ground black pepper

If there is one tinned food that I absolutely love, it would have to be tuna. This recipe is a mixture of flavours and colours that will never bore you. Great for picnic food or to pack in your children's lunchbox. Fantastico when it's hot and still fantastic when it's cold. My only tip would be to use good-quality tinned tuna (stored in olive oil not brine).

Boil the potatoes in a large pan of salted water until soft. Drain, mash and tip into a large bowl and leave to cool. Add the bread, eggs, tuna, sun-dried tomatoes, garlic, parsley, salt and pepper, and mix well together. Add the lemon zest and a little juice and keep stirring until evenly combined.

Preheat the oven to 180°C/350°F/gas mark 4. Use your hands to make balls the size of snooker balls, flatten gently and coat in the breadcrumbs. Place the fishcakes on a tray lined with baking paper and bake in the oven for about 15 minutes or until golden brown.

Meanwhile, cook the green beans in boiling salted water until al dente. Drain and place in a large bowl with the sesame seeds. Dress with extra virgin olive oil, a squeeze of lemon and season with salt.

Once the fishcakes are cooked, serve them with the crunchy green beans and enjoy with your friends.

This is probably the most versatile chapter in this book. Here you will find recipes from exciting salads to barbecue dishes. Being brought up in the south of Italy gave me the chance to understand the importance of choosing healthy and tasty ingredients and I strongly believe that the secret of a healthy dish is in the simplicity of the cooking. Rely on good-quality ingredients, tasty dressings and fantastic flavours.

Cooking tips

1. Choose a recipe with seasonal ingredients – it will be much healthier, colourful and usually cheaper

2. Do not overcook – let the natural freshness of the flavours come through

3. If you choose a salad dish, do not dress it until the last minute otherwise the leaves will cook and go soggy

4. Salads are great as light meals or as accompaniments to meat and fish dishes, but never serve with a pasta, soup or risotto dish – the cold crunch of a salad will ruin the warm comfort of the hot dish

5. See my recipe for Schiacciata Toscana (page 137) for a great Tuscan-style bread to serve with your barbecue or salad

6. Barbecues are a simple cooking method. My only tip: don't place the grill too close to the coals

French Beans with Sun-dried Tomatoes, Feta and Mozzarella

44 INSALATA DI FAGIOLINI

Serves 4

400g fine French beans

70g sun-dried tomatoes in oil, drained and sliced

50g shelled walnuts

5 tablespoons extra virgin olive oil

1 tablespoon freshly squeezed lemon juice

130g feta cheese

2 buffalo Mozzarella balls, drained and cut into chunks

Salt and pepper

This recipe (like most of my recipes) happened by accident. I was hosting a barbecue party and a friend of mine challenged me to make something that resembled the colours of the Italian flag. I went to the fridge, got hold of everything green, white and red and came up with this masterpiece. Today, it has become one of my signature dishes among my friends and we still enjoy it at every barbecue party. Make sure that the French beans are not overcooked and use a good-quality buffalo Mozzarella.

Trim ½cm from both ends of the beans, then cook in a large pan of boiling salted water for about 5 minutes until al dente. Drain well and place in a large bowl.

Lightly toss the hot beans with the sun-dried tomatoes, walnuts, extra virgin olive oil and lemon juice. Season with salt and pepper and leave to cool.

Once the beans have cooled, crumble in the feta and gently mix in the Mozzarella. Serve immediately.

Spinach and Watercress Salad
with Bacon and Pears

INSALATA DI SPINACI

Serves 4

150g smoked streaky bacon rashers

2 ripe pears

130g young spinach leaves, trimmed

100g watercress, trimmed

FOR THE DRESSING

3 tablespoons extra virgin olive oil

2 teaspoons hazelnut oil

1 teaspoon wholegrain mustard

2 teaspoons white wine vinegar

2 tablespoons sesame seeds

Salt and pepper

Once again I find myself in a very lucky position, because I can use the best of Italy and the best of Britain to create something unique. The combination of spinach, bacon and pears is just exceptional. If you don't have pears, you can always use your favourite apples or even papayas.

Grill the bacon until crispy, then transfer to kitchen paper to drain any excess oil and roughly chop.

Halve the pears, remove the cores and thinly slice.

Whisk together the dressing ingredients in a medium bowl.

Place the spinach and watercress in a large salad bowl with the bacon and pears. Pour over the dressing and toss lightly. Serve with warm crusty bread.

Tuna and Mixed Bean Salad

Serves 4

150g dried cannellini beans

150g dried borlotti beans

10 tablespoons extra virgin olive oil

5 tablespoons freshly squeezed lemon juice

400g tinned tuna in oil

2 medium red onions, sliced

2 garlic cloves, finely sliced

3 tablespoons roughly chopped flat-leaf parsley

Salt and pepper

Even today I have no idea which region in Italy this recipe comes from and, to be honest with you, it doesn't make any difference, because I would love it anyway. I often use beans in my salads, but this recipe is definitely my favourite one. If you don't want to soak dried beans, you can always use tinned ones, but just ensure that you drain the juice and rinse the beans under cold water. For best results, use good-quality tuna — one that has been tinned in olive or sunflower oil, never brine.

Put the beans in a large bowl, cover with cold water and leave to soak overnight.

The following day, drain the beans, place in a saucepan and cover with fresh water. Bring to the boil, then reduce the heat and cook, covered, for about 45 minutes until tender. Drain.

Whisk the extra virgin olive oil and the lemon juice together in a large bowl, season with salt and pepper and gently fold in the warm beans. Set aside to cool.

Drain the tuna and very gently flake the fish into the cooled beans. Lightly stir in the onions, garlic and parsley, adjust the seasoning and serve with your favourite bread.

Northern Italian Salad with Roasted Red Peppers

PANZANELLA

Serves 4

3 red peppers

2 tablespoons olive oil

1 small country-style loaf, cut into chunks

100g frisée lettuce

100g radicchio

1 small cucumber, cut into 1cm cubes

1 large red onion, finely sliced

3 ripe tomatoes, roughly chopped

2 tablespoons capers in vinegar

10 fresh basil leaves, roughly sliced

8 anchovy fillets in oil, drained and chopped

FOR THE DRESSING

3 tablespoons red wine vinegar

5 tablespoons extra virgin olive oil

1 teaspoon sugar

Salt and pepper

An authentic northern Italian salad full of flavour, crunchiness and colour. For perfection, try to use bread which is at least 2–3 days old. The beautiful thing about this salad is that you can add or take away any ingredient that you don't like, but believe you me when I tell you that I'm sure you will love it just the way it is. Remember to always dress the salad just before you serve it.

Preheat the oven to 180º/350°F/gas mark 4. Place the whole peppers in a large roasting tin with the olive oil and roast for about 20 minutes until the skins are blackened all over. Remove from the oven, place in a large bowl and cover with clingfilm.

Meanwhile, scatter the bread in a large roasting tin and toast in the oven for about 10 minutes or until golden and crisp.

Mix together the salad leaves, cucumber, onion, tomatoes, capers, basil and anchovies in a large bowl. Mix together the dressing ingredients, and add to the bowl, stirring to coat.

Remove the skin, stalk and seeds from the roasted peppers and cut the flesh into strips. Add to the salad bowl, along with the warm bread. Stir well and serve immediately.

Parma Ham with Minted Citrus Salad and Limoncello

Serves 4

2 papayas

1 small cantaloupe melon

1 grapefruit

1 ugli fruit (if you can't find ugli fruit, use pink grapefruit instead)

3 tablespoons finely sliced fresh mint leaves

2 tablespoons Limoncello liqueur

12 slices Parma ham

Fresh mint sprigs, to garnish

A wonderful, stylish recipe with refreshing flavours and fantastic colours. I guarantee that you will impress your friends with the Limoncello and fresh mint dressing. A great dish to prepare if you have a lot of guests coming for dinner. If you don't like Limoncello, you can always use Cointreau.

Peel the papayas, halve and remove the seeds. Slice the flesh and place in a large bowl.

Halve the melon and scoop out the seeds. Use a melon baller to scoop out the flesh and add to the bowl, along with the juice.

Use a sharp serrated knife to peel and segment the grapefruit and ugli fruit, discarding all the white pith – hold the fruit over the bowl to catch the juices.

Add the mint and Limoncello and lightly toss together.

Cover and chill for 30 minutes to allow the flavours to blend.

To serve, form a loose nest with three slices of Parma ham in the centre of each serving plate and fill the nest with the citrus salad in the middle. Garnish with the mint sprigs.

The Ultimate Warm Salad

Serves 4

200g new potatoes, unpeeled

8 quail's eggs

8 slices Parma ham

70g frisée lettuce

70g radicchio

50g white cabbage, shredded

150g pitted Kalamata olives

100g shelled walnuts

300g tuna chunks in oil, drained

70g Pecorino cheese, freshly shaved

FOR THE DRESSING

3 tablespoons apple cider vinegar or white wine vinegar

6 tablespoons extra virgin olive oil

1 tablespoon sherry liqueur

Salt and pepper

I often really fancy a good, tasty salad, but sometimes they can be quite boring. I like this one because of the contrast of flavours and especially the contrast between cold and warm ingredients. The saltiness of the Parma ham against the sweetness of the eggs works beautifully.

Cook the potatoes in a large saucepan of boiling salted water until al dente. Drain, cut in half and set aside.

Boil the eggs for 5 minutes. Peel and halve the eggs while still warm and set aside. Preheat the grill.

Place the Parma ham on a baking tray and grill for about 2 minutes on each side until crispy.

Put the salad leaves and cabbage into a large bowl. Add the olives, walnuts, tuna, the warm potatoes, crisp Parma ham and warm eggs. Season with salt and pepper.

Mix together the dressing ingredients in a small bowl. Season with salt and pepper, then pour over the salad and toss lightly.

Pile the salad onto a large serving plate, sprinkle the Pecorino shavings on top and serve immediately with warm crusty bread.

Griddled Lamb with Rosemary, Garlic and Courgettes

Serves 4

15 large garlic cloves, unpeeled

8 lamb loin chops (about 130g each)

8 long rosemary sprigs

6 medium courgettes, halved lengthways

Olive oil, for brushing

Salt and pepper

If you like lamb and Italian food, it is impossible not to like this recipe, as it sums up what Italian food is all about.

Drop the garlic into boiling salted water and cook for 5 minutes. Drain and set aside to cool.

Use a skewer to make a hole lengthways through each chop. Remove the skewer and thread with rosemary sprigs. Brush the meat and courgettes with olive oil.

Heat a griddle pan and start cooking the chops on one side for 5 minutes. Turn the chops and add the garlic and courgettes to the pan too. Griddle for a further 8 minutes, turning the vegetables every 2 minutes. Season, then transfer everything to a large flat tray to rest for 30 seconds.

Arrange three slices of courgette in the centre of each serving plate, scatter the charred garlic around it and arrange two chops on top of the courgettes. Serve immediately.

Barbecued Citrus and Honey Chicken Drumsticks

COSCETTE DI POLLO AL MIELE

Serves 4

16 chicken drumsticks (skin on) or pork ribs, if you prefer

FOR THE MARINADE

5 tablespoons runny honey

5 tablespoons dark soy sauce

Zest and juice of 2 unwaxed lemons

Zest and juice of 2 oranges

1 teaspoon paprika

Every time I have a barbecue, my two boys Luciano and Rocco ask me to prepare this. They not only love to eat this dish, but they love to help me prepare it because they can get their hands dirty, coating the drumsticks in the marinade.

Mix together the ingredients for the marinade in a large bowl.

With a sharp knife score the drumsticks and place in the bowl with the marinade. Cover and leave to marinate in the fridge for 2 hours, turning the chicken occasionally.

Meanwhile, preheat the barbecue and bring the chicken to room temperature. Cook the drumsticks for about 20 minutes, turning frequently and brushing with the marinade. Serve hot with a salad.

Poussin with Peperonata and Mozzarella

POLLETTO CON PEPERONATA

Serves 4

4 poussin

FOR THE MARINADE

4 teaspoons English mustard

4 tablespoons olive oil

1 glass red wine

5 tablespoons fresh rosemary, stripped from stalks

½ onion, sliced

Salt and pepper

FOR THE PEPERONATA

5 tablespoons olive oil

1 garlic clove, finely sliced

800g tinned or jarred roasted peppers, drained and sliced

1 tablespoon capers in salt, rinsed

100g pitted Kalamata olives

1 tablespoon chopped flat-leaf parsley

2 Mozzarella balls, drained and sliced

8 wooden skewers, presoaked in water

This recipe definitely shows the carnivorous side of me. I don't think that there is anything better in this world than to cook a whole poussin on the barbecue. I love using my fingers and eating the meat off the bones, experiencing all the flavours and textures and, of course, served with roasted peppers and melted Mozzarella, it becomes the ultimate meal. You can always substitute poussin for quails or pigeon. Perfect with a glass of dry Italian red wine.

Clean the poussin and use a sharp knife to cut along the backbone. Spatchcock the birds by flattening them down on a chopping board and inserting two crossed skewers through the centre of each bird to keep them flat. Transfer to a deep-sided baking tray.

Mix together the marinade ingredients in a large bowl. Pour over the poussin, cover with clingfilm and place in the fridge to marinate for about 20 minutes.

Meanwhile, preheat the barbecue or griddle pan and bring the poussin to room temperature. Transfer the poussin to the barbecue or griddle and cook for about 7 minutes on each side.

Heat 3 tablespoons of the olive oil in a medium saucepan and gently fry the garlic until golden, then add the peppers, capers and olives. Season with salt and pepper, stir well and simmer over a medium heat for about 5 minutes. Stir in the parsley and cook for a further 5 minutes.

Place the pepper mixture in a dish measuring 20 x 10cm and cover with the sliced Mozzarella. Drizzle with the remaining olive oil, grind over some black pepper and grill for about 5 minutes or until golden and melted. Serve the poussin with the peperonata.

Marinated Seafood Skewers

Serves 4

130g shelled scampi
(langoustines)

400g shelled scallops (with
corals)

150g salmon steak, cut into
pieces the size of the scallops

150g tuna steak, cut into pieces
the size of the scallops

2 lemons, cut into wedges, to
serve

FOR THE MARINADE

6 tablespoons olive oil

Zest and juice of 1 unwaxed
lemon

1 tablespoon chopped fresh
oregano

1 teaspoon fennel seeds

Salt and pepper

This recipe was created by my mother and I remember she always used to prepare these marinated seafood skewers in the summer. I guess one of the reasons she did this was because they were very easy to prepare and very quick to cook. Of course, if you don't want to cook them on a barbecue, you can always cook them under a hot grill for the same amount of time.

First make the marinade. Whisk the olive oil with the lemon zest and juice in a large bowl. Add the oregano and fennel seeds and season with salt and pepper.

Skewer the seafood and fish alternately onto four metal skewers and place in a shallow dish measuring 35 x 20cm. Pour over the marinade, cover and chill in the fridge for 2 hours, turning frequently.

Preheat the barbecue or grill and bring the fish skewers back to room temperature. Remove the skewers from the marinade and cook on the hot barbecue or under the grill for about 6 minutes, turning and basting frequently with the remaining marinade.

Serve immediately on a bed of crisp salad leaves with the lemon wedges.

Pasta This is a subject I can talk about forever. I have been eating pasta since I can remember and a plate of pasta is to me the ultimate comfort food. Have a look at Veg Out (page 110) for some fantastic veggie pasta dishes.

Cooking tips on pasta. OK, where do I start...

1. To cook the perfect pasta, you should always ensure that you have enough water in the pan (500g dried pasta to 2.5 litres of water)
2. Make sure that the water is always fast boiling before you start cooking
3. The water should always be salted
4. Never cook pasta with the lid on
5. Keep tasting as you cook, ensuring the pasta remains al dente (firm to the bite)
6. ALWAYS put the pasta into the sauce NEVER the sauce on top of the pasta!
7. THE MOST IMPORTANT RULE OF ALL: never add cheese to seafood or fish pasta!

Soups I must admit I appreciate soups much more now than I have ever done before. When I lived in Napoli, we never ate soup, as it is hot there for most of the year. The closest we came to it was bean soup, but now living in London, there is nothing better than a tasty soup with some warm crusty bread.

The secret to a good soup? Only one tip.

1. Endless combinations of ingredients that you like – anything goes

Risotto

In my opinion, making a risotto is the only way of doing justice to a simple grain of rice. The most popular rice used in Italy is Arborio, which you will recognise by its short grain essential for an authentic risotto. The thing I like most about a risotto is that it is a meal in itself and can be as versatile as you want. I still can't believe how many people are afraid of preparing risotto and have difficulty in getting the consistency right.

Like everything else in life there are rules to follow...

1. If you can't find risotto rice (Arborio and Carnaroli are the most common), DON'T use anything else. It won't work
2. Always cook the risotto in a large saucepan
3. Never cook the risotto with the lid on
4. Toast the rice in the saucepan before adding any stock
5. Always stir the risotto with a wooden spoon
6. When adding stock, always ensure that it is well absorbed before adding any more
7. Never leave the pan alone while cooking the risotto (keep stirring)
8. If you want to add cheese, it should always be added at the end, but do not ever add cheese to a seafood or fish risotto
9. If you want a creamy finish, stir in a couple of knobs of butter with the cheese

Seafood and Asparagus Risotto

Serves 4

150g thin asparagus stalks

150g fresh mussels

5 tablespoons olive oil

1 onion, finely chopped

350g Arborio rice

Pinch of saffron powder or strands

100ml dry white wine

1.2 litres warm fish stock (made from 2 fish stock cubes)

150g fresh raw prawns, peeled, heads and tails removed

100g large scallops with the coral, cut in half

Zest of 1 small unwaxed lemon

80g salted butter

Salt and pepper

For anyone who likes seafood, this is the recipe to try because the combination of saffron, asparagus, rice and seafood works perfectly. I wish my grandfather was still here to try it, because he loved risotto with seafood. Please make sure you use fresh mussels and if they are not in season, leave out the asparagus.

Cut off the tips of the asparagus and peel the stalks. Cut into 4cm lengths and set aside.

Place the mussels in the sink, and under cold running water, scrape off any grit. With your fingers, pull away the hairy beards that protrude from the shells. Using the back of a knife, tap any mussels that remain open, and if they refuse to close, throw them away. Rinse again in cold water until there is no trace of sand. Set aside.

Heat the olive oil in a large saucepan and fry the onion on a medium heat for about 2 minutes or until softened. Add in the asparagus stalks and continue to cook for a further 3 minutes, stirring continuously.

Add the rice and, using a wooden spoon, keep stirring for 3 minutes, allowing the rice to toast in the oil and begin to absorb all the flavours.

Add in the saffron and the wine and continue to cook for a further 3 minutes to allow the alcohol to evaporate.

Start to add the warm stock a little at a time, season and cook gently, stirring until the stock is absorbed. Continue adding the stock as each addition is absorbed. If you need to, add more warm water to the stock.

Just before most of the stock has been absorbed (about 15 minutes), add in the prawns, scallops, mussels, lemon zest and asparagus tips, and continue to cook for a further 5 minutes.

When the risotto is ready, take the saucepan off the heat and add the butter. It is very important that you stir the butter into the rice for at least 1 minute so you can create a fantastic creamy texture. Serve immediately.

Three-mushroom Risotto with Peas

Serves 4

5 tablespoons olive oil

1 medium onion, finely chopped

100g portobello mushrooms, sliced

80g chestnut mushrooms, sliced

20g sliced dried Porcini mushrooms, soaked in cold water for 30 minutes to soften

150g frozen peas, thawed

400g Arborio or Carnaroli rice

100ml dry white wine

1 tablespoon fresh thyme leaves

1.2 litres warm vegetable stock, made with 2 stock cubes

50g salted butter

100g freshly grated Parmesan cheese

Salt and pepper

Once when I was cooking for my wife and her girlfriends, they all described this dish as warm and comforting, like a cuddle. Of course, I thought that this was my lucky night, but once the risotto was finished, I was ditched. When in season, substitute the dry Porcini for fresh ones (150g) and use good-quality rice for perfect results. Don't be afraid to make this dish; remember it's a one-pot dish and if you follow my instructions, you will actually find it quite easy.

Heat the olive oil in a large saucepan and fry the onion over a medium heat for about 2 minutes or until softened. Add in all the mushrooms and the peas and continue to cook for a further 3 minutes. Add the rice and stir continuously using a wooden spoon for 5 minutes to allow the rice to toast in the olive oil and begin to absorb all the mushroom flavours. Add the wine and continue to cook for a further 3 minutes to allow the alcohol to evaporate.

Add the thyme and the warm stock a little at a time, stirring occasionally, allowing the rice to absorb the stock before adding more. Season well and cook gently (if you need extra liquid, use warm water).

After about 20 minutes, when most of the stock has been absorbed, remove the pan from the heat and stir the butter into the risotto. It is very important that you stir the butter very fast into the rice for at least 1 minute – this creates a fantastic creamy texture.

Add the Parmesan and serve immediately.

Deep-fried Risotto Balls Served with Spicy Tomato Sauce

Serves 6

5 tablespoons olive oil

1 onion, finely chopped

500g Arborio or Carnaroli rice

1 litre warm vegetable stock

100ml passata (sieved tomatoes)

100g frozen peas, thawed

150g freshly grated Parmesan cheese

3 medium eggs, separated

200g toasted fine breadcrumbs

200g Mozzarella cheese, drained and cubed

1 litre vegetable oil, for deep-frying

Salt and pepper

FOR THE SAUCE

5 tablespoons olive oil

1 garlic clove, finely sliced

1 large hot chilli, deseeded and sliced

300g fresh plum tomatoes, chopped, skin and seeds included

Salt

Every Sunday my father used to take me around the town of Torre del Greco where I was born. We used to do our weekly shop in the markets and we would eat this in the middle of the road or sitting on the step of a church. Forget about burgers or hotdogs, this is the ultimate Neapolitan street food. The preparation will take at least one hour but once cooked, the rice balls are great to serve at parties.

Heat the olive oil in a large saucepan, and gently fry the onion until golden. Add the rice and continue to fry for about 3 minutes, stirring constantly with a wooden spoon.

Add the vegetable stock a little at a time, allowing the rice to absorb the stock before adding more (if you need extra, use warm water) and cook for about 20 minutes, stirring constantly. Season with salt and pepper, add the passata, the peas, the Parmesan and the egg yolks. Mix well then spread out the risotto on a tray and leave to cool.

Lightly beat the egg whites (you only want to break up the yolks) and spread the breadcrumbs on a plate. Once the risotto is cooled, place about 3 large tablespoons of rice in the centre of your hand (wet your hands in cold water so the rice doesn't stick to them) and roll the rice into a ball about the size of a snooker ball. Press some Mozzarella in the centre and form the rice into a ball again. Dip in the egg whites and cover with breadcrumbs. Repeat with the remaining risotto and Mozzarella. Put the rice balls on a tray and leave in the fridge for about 1 hour.

While the rice balls are resting, prepare the sauce. Heat the olive oil in a saucepan and fry the garlic and chilli until golden. Add the tomatoes, season with salt and cook over a medium heat for about 10 minutes.

Heat enough vegetable oil in a heavy-based saucepan to ensure that the rice balls can be completely submerged. Roll the rice balls in the breadcrumbs for a second time.

Deep-fry the balls for about 2 minutes or until golden (work in batches, if necessary), then transfer to kitchen paper to allow any excess oil to drain.

To serve, pour all the sauce in the centre of a large serving plate and place the rice balls on top, ready to be shared with your friends.

Pasta with Prawns and Rocket

LINGUINE AI GAMBERI E RUCOLA

Serves 4

5 tablespoons olive oil

2 garlic cloves, finely sliced

50g pine nuts

1 medium-hot red chilli, finely sliced and deseeded

300g large fresh raw prawns, peeled, heads and tails removed

½ glass dry white wine

3 tablespoons finely sliced fresh basil

500g linguine

100g rocket leaves

Salt

This is one of my signature dishes, created in the summer of 2003 on the island of Sardinia where my family and I were enjoying our holiday in our house on the beach. Make sure that you serve this dish as soon as you combine the pasta and the sauce. You can substitute the prawns for scallops.

Heat the olive oil in a large frying pan and shallow-fry the garlic, pine nuts and chilli for about 20 seconds, then add the prawns and cook for about 1 minute. Add the wine and basil, season with salt and simmer over a high heat for about 2 minutes. Remove the pan from the heat.

Meanwhile, cook the pasta in a large pan of boiling salted water until al dente. Drain and add to the frying pan. Return the frying pan to a high heat and immediately add in the rocket leaves, mix well for about 1 minute to allow the rocket to soften slightly and the pasta to absorb the flavour. Serve immediately.

Pasta Bows with Smoked Salmon and Peas

FARFALLE SALMONE E PISELLI

Serves 4

70g salted butter

1 tablespoon olive oil

3 shallots, finely chopped

150g frozen peas, thawed

100g smoked salmon, chopped

100ml single cream

500g farfalle

Salt and pepper

When I was a child, smoked salmon was always a treat for us, because at the time it was quite expensive and my mother would only make this dish once a month. To this day, I still love it.

Melt the butter and oil in a large frying pan and gently shallow-fry the shallots until golden. Add the peas and cook for about 3 minutes. Add the salmon, check the seasoning (be careful as smoked salmon is quite salty), and cook over a medium heat for a further 3 minutes. Add in the cream and cook for 2–3 minutes or until it starts to thicken slightly.

Meanwhile, cook the pasta in a large pan of boiling salted water until al dente. Drain and immediately add to the sauce. Mix well over a medium heat, stirring constantly to ensure the sauce coats the pasta beautifully. Serve immediately with freshly ground pepper on top.

Baked Pasta with Four-cheese Sauce and Salame

Serves 4

500g penne rigate

80g salted butter

200g cream cheese

100g Gorgonzola cheese, cubed

100g grated Cheddar cheese

½ glass full-fat milk at room temperature

150g salame Milano, in small dice

3 tablespoons roughly chopped flat-leaf parsley

70g freshly grated Parmesan cheese

Whenever I think about this recipe, I think comfort food. It is impossible not to like this dish (unless you don't like cheese). You can substitute some of the cheeses for your favourite ones and, without the salame, it will make a great vegetarian dish.

Cook the pasta in a large pan of boiling salted water until al dente, bearing in mind it will also cook in the oven. Drain and return to the saucepan. Add the butter and the cheeses except the Parmesan. Mix well using a wooden spoon and slowly add in the milk. Stir constantly over a medium heat until the cheeses are melted and you have a creamy texture. Add in the salame, season and stir in the parsley.

Preheat the oven to 180°C/350°F/gas mark 4. Spoon the pasta mixture into a large baking tray (35 x 20 x 7cm), sprinkle over the Parmesan and bake in the centre of the oven for 15 minutes or until the top is golden and crisp. Serve immediately.

Pasta with Ham and Mushrooms in Cream

TAGLIATELLE PANNA E PROSCIUTTO

Serves 4

100g salted butter

200g button mushrooms, sliced

200g cooked ham, thickly sliced then cut into small squares

300ml single cream

Pinch of grated nutmeg

500g fresh tagliatelle

100g freshly grated Parmesan cheese

Salt and pepper

If you aren't watching your weight and you want to cook a very quick, easy and extremely tasty pasta dish, this is the recipe to choose. The combination of ingredients is classic and you really can't go wrong.

Melt the butter in a large frying pan and fry the mushrooms and ham over a medium heat for 10 minutes or until golden. Add the cream, season with salt, pepper and a pinch of nutmeg and cook, uncovered, for about 2 minutes.

Meanwhile, cook the pasta in a large pan of boiling salted water until al dente. Drain and immediately add to the sauce. Stir constantly, allowing the sauce to thicken slightly. Serve at once with plenty of Parmesan on top.

Spaghetti Rolled in Aubergines
with Melted Cheese

INVOLTINI DI MELANZANE E SPAGHETTI

Serves 4

2 whole aubergines

5 tablespoons olive oil

1 garlic cloves, chopped

500g tinned chopped tomatoes

10 fresh basil leaves

350g spaghetti

Butter, for greasing

2 Mozzarella balls, drained and sliced

100g freshly grated Pecorino cheese

Extra virgin olive oil

Salt and pepper

This is definitely a wow plate of pasta. Simple flavours, a bit fiddly to put together, but believe me you will enjoy every minute of it. A dish that you can prepare at least half an hour before your guests arrive and no need to accompany anything with it. You can serve it as a starter or main course and, if you don't want to use spaghetti, you can always use linguine. My tip would be not to overcook the pasta and make sure that the aubergines are cooked enough, otherwise they can get very leathery.

Slice the aubergines in lengths about 1cm thick. Place in a large sieve, sprinkle with salt and leave for about 30 minutes to allow the excess water to drain. Carefully dry each slice on kitchen paper.

Heat a griddle pan and cook the aubergines for about 3 minutes on each side, then set aside and leave to cool.

Heat the olive oil in a medium saucepan, gently fry the garlic until golden, then add the chopped tomatoes. Season and leave to simmer, uncovered, for 15 minutes, stirring occasionally. Remove from the heat, mix in the basil and leave the sauce to become tepid.

Meanwhile, bring a large pan of salted water to the boil and cook the spaghetti until al dente according to the packet instructions. Drain and mix into the tomato sauce to allow the pasta to absorb the flavours.

Preheat the oven to 200°C/400°F/gas mark 6. Place a slice of grilled aubergine on a greased baking tray measuring about 30 x 20cm and spoon some of the pasta in the middle. Add a slice of Mozzarella, roll up the aubergine and secure with a toothpick. Repeat the process until all the ingredients are used up.

Sprinkle the rolls with Pecorino and bake in the centre of the oven for 10 minutes.

Once the cheese has melted, drizzle with extra virgin olive oil, remove the toothpicks and serve immediately.

Pasta Shells with Spicy Sprouting Broccoli and Purple Basil

ORECCHIETTE CON BROCCOLETTI

Serves 4

6 tablespoons olive oil

200g sprouting broccoli

2 garlic cloves, finely sliced

1 medium red chilli, deseeded and finely sliced

100ml dry white wine

500g orecchiette pasta

100g freshly grated Pecorino cheese

5 tablespoons toasted pine nuts

10 purple basil leaves

Salt

This is an authentic traditional dish that comes from the region of Puglia in southern Italy. To be precise, it comes from a town called Bari where they are absolutely mad about orecchiette pasta. The translation of the shape of the pasta in English is little pretty ears, which of course doesn't sound very appetising, but trust me the flavour of the garlic, with the spiciness of the chilli and the crunchiness of the broccoli will send you straight to heaven (aren't I a poet!) Try not to but if you have to, you can substitute Pecorino cheese for Parmesan and if you can't find the orecchiette, use any shell-shaped pasta.

Heat the olive oil in a large wok and stir-fry the broccoli with the garlic and the chilli over a high heat for 3 minutes. Season with salt, add the white wine and continue to cook over a medium heat for a further 8 minutes. Make sure that the broccoli stays al dente.

Meanwhile, cook the pasta in boiling salted water until al dente. Drain and add to the wok. Increase the heat to high and add the Pecorino, pine nuts and basil. Toss well for 1 minute allowing all the flavours to combine with the pasta. Serve immediately.

Pasta with Meat Sauce and Parmesan Cheese

Serves 4

4 tablespoons olive oil

1 onion, finely chopped

450g minced beef

100ml red wine

600g passata (sieved tomatoes)

2 tablespoons sun-dried tomato paste or red pesto

100g frozen peas, thawed

4 tablespoons full-fat milk

400g fresh tagliatelle

100g freshly grated Parmesan cheese

Salt and pepper

I wanted to write a traditional bolognese recipe but to make such a recipe, you need more than 25 ingredients and 18 hours of cooking time. So I decided to create a meat sauce that is quicker to make but still with fabulous flavours. Every time my friends come round to watch football, I make this dish and it always goes down well, especially with a cold beer. You can substitute the minced beef for minced lamb, and you can use penne pasta instead of tagliatelle.

Heat the oil in a large saucepan and fry the onion over a medium heat until soft.

Add in the minced beef and fry for about 8 minutes, stirring constantly.

Add in the wine, stir well and continue to cook for a further 5 minutes, to allow the alcohol to evaporate.

Pour in the passata together with the sun-dried tomato paste and the peas and stir well. Half cover with the lid and cook over a low heat for 30 minutes, stirring occasionally.

Stir in the milk, season and allow to rest for 5 minutes.

In the meantime, cook the pasta in a large saucepan with plenty of boiling salted water until al dente.

Drain the pasta and add immediately to the sauce. Stir for 1 minute so that the pasta absorbs the flavours. Serve straightaway, with plenty of Parmesan cheese on top.

Leek, Potato and Rocket Soup

Serves 6

60g salted butter

1 onion, chopped

2 medium King Edward potatoes, diced

3 large leeks, chopped

900ml warm chicken stock

150g rocket leaves, roughly chopped

1 ciabatta loaf, halved lengthways

2 garlic cloves

150ml double cream

Salt and white pepper

One of my favourite British recipes has to be leek and potato soup. Such a simple recipe but with a unique balance of flavours. I decided to add rocket leaves to this fantastic soup, which adds a peppery flavour to the dish. Do serve this soup with my home-made garlic croûtons, you are going to love it! Make sure that the consistency of the soup is not too runny and use fresh leeks for best results.

Melt the butter in a large saucepan, add the onion, potatoes and leeks and stir to coat the vegetables in butter. Continue to fry over a medium heat for about 10 minutes until the vegetables start to soften. Pour in the stock and bring to the boil, then reduce the heat and cook, covered, for 20 minutes.

Pass the soup through a food mill and return to the rinsed-out pan. (Do not blitz the soup in a food-processor, as this gives the soup a gluey texture.) Add the rocket to the pan and cook, uncovered, over a medium heat for a further 6 minutes, stirring occasionally.

Meanwhile, toast the ciabatta halves under a grill until crisp and brown. Leave to cool slightly, then rub all over with the garlic cloves and cut into 2cm cubes.

Stir the cream into the soup, season with salt and pepper and ladle into warmed soup bowls. Serve immediately with a few garlic ciabatta croûtons on top.

Minestrone

Serves 6

5 tablespoons olive oil

2 onions, diced

2 carrots, peeled and diced

2 celery sticks, washed and diced

200g tinned cannellini beans, drained

300g King Edward potatoes, peeled and diced

200g dark green cabbage, roughly chopped

400g tinned chopped tomatoes

200g French beans, diced

2 litres vegetable stock, made with 4 stock cubes

120g conchigliette (baby shells)

4 tablespoons roughly chopped flat-leaf parsley

80g freshly grated Parmesan cheese

Salt and pepper

Every Italian cookery book has to have a minestrone recipe in it and this is the way I cook it – very light and the ingredients I have chosen don't need to be cooked for a long time. My children absolutely love this soup – if you have children, don't be scared to let them try this, it's a great way to get vegetables inside them without an argument. A great starter and accompanied with some fresh crusty bread, it also makes a fantastic and filling main course. My tip would be not to overcook it, otherwise the bright colours and the crunchiness of the vegetables will disappear.

Heat the olive oil in a large saucepan over a medium heat and fry the onions, carrots and celery for about 10 minutes or until golden.

Add the cannellini beans, potatoes, cabbage, chopped tomatoes, French beans and stock and bring to the boil. Season to taste. Reduce the heat, half cover the pan with the lid and cook for 30 minutes.

Remove the lid, add the pasta with the parsley and continue to cook over a medium heat for a further 25 minutes, stirring occasionally.

Check that all the vegetables are tender and the pasta is cooked, and serve immediately sprinkled with plenty of Parmesan.

Spicy Bean Soup with Pancetta and Sausages

Serves 6

5 tablespoons olive oil

3 garlic cloves, crushed

3 tablespoons fresh rosemary, stripped from stalks

200g pancetta, finely chopped

2 carrots, peeled and diced

1 celery stick, washed and diced

3 teaspoons dry chilli flakes

4 pork sausages, sliced into 2cm chunks

400g tinned cannellini beans, drained

400g tinned borlotti beans, drained

400g tinned chickpeas, drained

400g tinned green lentils, drained

500ml vegetable stock

80g freshly shaved Pecorino cheese

Salt and pepper

In May 2005, I was lucky enough to travel around Mexico filming a cookery series and this recipe was influenced by my time there. An earthy and rustic dish with a chilli kick, it will warm you in an instant. It's also a beautiful dish to make when you have loads of guests coming round and will save you washing up. Try to get good-quality sausages for a better result and my tip would be to let the casserole rest before serving, allowing all the flavours to develop.

Heat the olive oil in a large saucepan and fry the garlic, rosemary, pancetta, carrots, celery, chilli and sausage over a high heat for about 10 minutes or until golden brown.

Add all the beans and lentils with the stock. Bring to the boil. Season to taste, then reduce the heat, half cover the pan with the lid and cook for 30 minutes, stirring occasionally.

Remove from the heat and leave to rest for 10 minutes. Serve with freshly shaved Pecorino and your favourite crusty bread.

SOMETHING FISHY

Every day I hear people telling me that they are absolutely scared of cooking fish. Of course, it's very difficult for me to understand this, because I was born on the Napoli coast and so was brought up predominantly on a fish diet. I find cooking fish much easier than cooking meat or vegetables — if you buy a fresh piece of fish, there really is not much cooking involved.

   If this is your first attempt at cooking fish, I would recommend Involtini di Pesce alle Olive (page 88), because it's easy to prepare and full of flavour.

Cooking tips

1. Do not overcook the fish — it should be flaky and not dry
2. The fish is ready when the bones can be pulled out easily
3. Never never never use a strong cheese as it will overpower the fish
4. When you buy fish, always smell it — if it's too fishy, it's not fresh
5. Fresh fish from your fishmonger will definitely taste better than supermarket produce and the fishmonger will usually prepare it for you, too
6. If you are having a dinner party, impress them with Spigola in Barchetta (page 93)
7. A fish dish should always be served as soon as it's been cooked
8. Please make sure that your fish comes from sustainable sources and is caught using environmentally responsible fishing methods

Crispy Fillet of Salmon with Cherry Tomato and Anchovy Sauce

Serves 2

2 medium eggs

2 tablespoons chopped flat-leaf parsley

100g toasted fine breadcrumbs

2 teaspoons coarse sea salt

50g plain flour

2 medium salmon or plaice fillets (about 120g each)

FOR THE SAUCE

200ml olive oil

½ red onion, finely sliced

4 anchovy fillets in oil, drained

400g tinned cherry tomatoes

3 tablespoons finely chopped flat-leaf parsley

Salt and pepper

This is the kind of fish dish that I love to eat when I want something light, colourful and very very tasty. My grandfather used to make this recipe in his restaurant in Sardinia and it was probably his best-selling dish, but he used plaice instead of salmon. If you can't find tinned cherry tomatoes, you can use tinned chopped tomatoes. Make sure you use anchovies in oil and not the ones marinated in vinegar, otherwise they will be too sharp for the sauce. To prepare the breadcrumbs, cut some stale bread into chunks, roast in the oven until brown and crisp, and once cooled, blitz them very finely (see page 8).

Beat the eggs in a large bowl with the parsley and a pinch of salt. Mix the breadcrumbs, sea salt and flour together on a large plate. Dip the fish fillets into the egg mixture and coat in the breadcrumb mixture.

Heat 4 tablespoons of the olive oil in a medium saucepan and fry the onion until golden. Add the anchovies, cherry tomatoes and parsley, season with salt and pepper and cook, uncovered, over a medium heat for 10 minutes.

Meanwhile, heat the remaining oil in a large frying pan and gently fry the breaded fish for about 3 minutes on each side until golden and crisp. Transfer to kitchen paper to allow any excess oil to drain.

To serve, spread the cherry tomato sauce in the middle of two serving plates and place the crispy fish on top. Perfect with a glass of cold white wine.

Monkfish Roasted with Parma Ham and New Potatoes

CODA DI ROSPO AL PARMA

Serves 6

80g salted butter

2 medium onions, sliced

800g new potatoes, quartered

5 sprigs fresh thyme

2 garlic cloves

8 anchovy fillets in oil, drained

5 tablespoons finely chopped flat-leaf parsley

60g fresh white breadcrumbs

4 tablespoons olive oil

1kg monkfish tail, cut into 4 fillets (if you can't find monkfish, use cod instead)

16 slices Parma ham

Salt and pepper

This is a wonderful dish if you're looking for plenty of flavour, lots of food and very little washing up. As you can see from the recipe, it only needs a large baking tray and so is perfect for those busy people who still enjoy cooking. The Parma ham and anchovies will bring loads of flavour to the monkfish and, served with my roast potatoes, it makes a complete meal. If you have to, substitute the monkfish for fresh cod and you can definitely use rosemary instead of thyme. My tip would be to ensure you cook this dish in the middle of the oven for a better overall temperature.

Preheat the oven to 200°C/400°F/gas mark 6.

Grease a large roasting tray with half the butter and tip in the onions and potatoes. Season well with salt and pepper, sprinkle over half the thyme and dot with the remaining butter.

Roast in the middle of the oven for about 55 minutes or until golden and crisp (shake the tray every 10 minutes).

Meanwhile, place the garlic, anchovies, parsley and breadcrumbs in the bowl of a food-processor. Add 2 tablespoons of the olive oil, season with salt and pepper and process until well mixed. (If it looks dry, add extra olive oil.)

Lay two monkfish fillets flat-side up on a chopping board and sprinkle with the mixture. Place the remaining fillets on top to create two parcels. Wrap the Parma ham around each parcel and tie with fine string at 2cm intervals.

After 35 minutes, remove the tray from the oven, place the monkfish parcels on top of the potatoes and roast for a further 20 minutes.

To serve, transfer the potatoes and the fish onto a large serving plate, garnish with the rest of the thyme and enjoy immediately.

Fish Stew

Serves 6

6 tablespoons olive oil

1 large onion, finely chopped

5 anchovy fillets in oil, drained

1 red pepper, roasted, skinned, deseeded and sliced

200ml dry white wine

250ml fish stock

600g tinned chopped tomatoes

3 tablespoons finely chopped flat-leaf parsley

1 sachet of saffron powder (0.012g)

300g haddock, skinned and cut into large chunks

300g cod, skinned and cut into large chunks

300g red mullet, skinned and cut into large chunks

20 large raw prawns (shell on)

20 mussels, cleaned

Salt and pepper

No matter if it's winter or summer, spring or autumn, no dish will ever beat a good fish stew. After a long day or when you feel particularly tired, it will really give you the energy you need. An explosion of flavour with colour and texture that won't disappoint. It's also a great recipe to prepare in the afternoon ready to be served in the evening and it's often used in Italy as a starter with good warm crunchy bread. If you fancy it, you can substitute the red mullet for salmon and if you don't like mussels, you can always use fresh clams.

Heat the olive oil in a large saucepan and gently fry the onion, anchovies and pepper for about 5 minutes. Add the wine and cook for a further 2 minutes, allowing the alcohol to evaporate.

Stir in the fish stock with the tomatoes, parsley and saffron and season with salt and pepper. Bring to the boil, then reduce to a medium heat and cook, uncovered, for about 20 minutes.

Add in the fish, stir well and continue to cook for about 5 minutes. Add in the prawns and the mussels, cover and cook for a further 5 minutes over a medium heat or until the mussel shells have opened. (Discard any unopened ones.)

Transfer the stew to a large serving bowl and serve immediately.

Mixed Fried Fish

Serves 6

5 small red mullet, cleaned and filleted

200g sole, cleaned and filleted

150g haddock, cleaned and filleted

300g whitebait

600g squid, cleaned

100g plain flour, seasoned

15 large raw prawns, peeled

2 courgettes, sliced and cut into matchsticks

1 litre vegetable oil, for frying

2 lemons, cut into wedges

Salt and pepper

For anybody who isn't a big fan of fish, this is probably the safest way to introduce them to it. Let me give you an example. My best friend Marco says he absolutely hates fish and yet every time we go to Italy together, the only thing he seems to eat is Fritto Misto — because the fish has been fried in small chunks, he doesn't taste the stronger fishy flavours you get from cooking it any other way. Serve the fish with the courgettes because the balance works well. Ideal for dinner parties where you serve everything on one big platter — either as a main or a starter, but remember to salt the fish.

Cut the mullet, sole and haddock fillets into chunks. Slice the body of the squid into rings about ½cm thick. (If you have the tentacles of the squid, cut into 1cm pieces).

Place the flour on a large plate and toss all the fish, the prawns and the courgettes until well coated.

Heat the oil in a large wok and fry the fish, prawns and courgettes until crisp and golden brown, working in batches. Drain on kitchen paper and keep each batch warm while frying the remainder.

Place the fritto misto on a large serving plate and garnish with lemon wedges.

Fresh Sardines Stuffed with Ricotta and Herbs

SARDINE RIPIENE CON RICOTTA ED ERBE

Serves 4

12 fresh sardines, cleaned, gutted, heads and spines removed

6 large tomatoes, sliced

5 tablespoons olive oil

4 tablespoons extra virgin olive oil

Salt and pepper

FOR THE STUFFING

300g ricotta cheese

50g breadcrumbs

2 medium eggs

3 tablespoons finely chopped flat-leaf parsley

2 tablespoons finely chopped fresh chives

2 tablespoons capers in salt, rinsed and finely chopped

1 garlic clove, finely chopped

This is a traditional Sicilian dish usually made with sardines or anchovies. A perfect combination of soft cheese blended with fresh herbs complements the beautiful fish. I usually serve it as a main course, but it can also be a starter. If you don't want to use sardines, you can use fresh mackerel and you can substitute parsley for basil. As I suggest in the recipe, ensure you serve it on a bed of tomato salad to freshen your palate.

Wash the sardines in cold water and dry on kitchen paper. Open out and lay flat on a chopping board with the skin side down. Preheat the oven to 180°C/350°F/Gas Mark 4.

To prepare the stuffing, mix the ricotta, breadcrumbs, eggs, parsley, chives, capers and garlic in a large bowl to create a smooth paste. Season with salt and pepper.

Divide the mixture between half of the flattened sardines, spread and cover with another sardine, sandwich-fashion. Once they are ready, place on an oiled baking tray, drizzle with the remaining olive oil and cook in the oven for about 20 minutes.

Serve the sardines immediately on a bed of sliced tomatoes dressed with extra virgin olive oil, salt and pepper.

Devilled Oysters with Spicy Tomato Sauce

Serves 4

24 very fresh oysters

FOR THE SAUCE

10 tablespoons olive oil

2 garlic cloves, finely sliced

2 teaspoons dry chilli flakes

500g plum tomatoes, chopped, with seeds and skin

2 medium eggs

6 tablespoons finely chopped flat-leaf parsley

100g plain flour

150g toasted very fine breadcrumbs (see page 8)

Salt

I'm sure you've heard about food that acts as an aphrodisiac. Well, this is one of them! A dish that will definitely not disappoint your partner, in every sense of the word. My only advice would be not to eat this dish by yourself... You can use fresh chilli instead of the dry chilli flakes and, if you really don't like oysters, try it with fresh scallops.

To open the oysters, cover your hand with a tea-towel, hold the shell and insert the tip of a sharp knife into the muscle between the two halves. Remove the oyster and place on kitchen paper to dry.

To prepare the sauce, heat 3 tablespoons of the olive oil in a large frying pan and fry the garlic and chilli together until golden, then add the chopped tomatoes. Season with salt and cook over a low heat for about 10 minutes.

Mix the eggs with half the parsley in a large bowl and season with salt and pepper. Dust each oyster with flour, dip in the egg mixture, then coat in breadcrumbs.

Heat the remaining oil in a frying pan and gently fry the oysters for about 1 minute on each side.

To serve, put 4–5 tablespoons of the tomato sauce in the middle of each serving plate and arrange six oysters on top. Garnish with the remaining parsley and serve immediately with grissini (breadsticks) and a glass of chilled Italian Spumante.

Rolled Fillets of Plaice with Black Olive and Caper Dressing

INVOLTINI DI PESCE ALLE OLIVE

Serves 4

8 plaice fillets (about 80g each), skinned (or sea bass or Dover sole)

100g black olive paste or tapenade

160ml dry white wine

2 large plum tomatoes, deseeded and diced

50g pitted Kalamata olives, finely sliced

FOR THE DRESSING

Zest and juice of 1 unwaxed lemon

2 tablespoons capers in salt, rinsed

5 tablespoons extra virgin olive oil

10 fresh basil leaves

Salt and pepper

This is a perfect example of a dish from the region of Calabria, in southern Italy. Like the Neapolitans, they believe in fresh produce with a few tasty and simple ingredients. You could also try this dish with sea bass or Dover sole. If you don't like black olive paste, substitute it for green olive paste or sun-dried tomato paste. Please ensure you buy good-quality black olives – remember, the colour of a good black olive should never be black but the colour of an aubergine.

Lay the fillets of plaice on a chopping board skinned-side up and spread with the black olive paste. Roll them up and secure with cocktail sticks.

Place the rolled fish in a deep-sided frying pan and pour over the wine. Gently bring to the boil. Reduce the heat, cover and simmer for about 10 minutes. Do not season, because the black olive paste is salty.

Put 4 tablespoons of the cooking liquor from the fish in a large bowl with the tomatoes and olives. Make the dressing by adding in the lemon zest and juice, the capers, olive oil, then season with salt and pepper. Mix the dressing with a spoon, stirring to coat the tomatoes and olives.

Transfer the fish to a warmed serving dish using a slotted spoon and pour over the dressing. Garnish with fresh basil leaves.

Grilled Turbot with Basil
and Tomato Cream Sauce

Serves 4

8 turbot steaks (about 80g each)

FOR THE SAUCE

300ml full-fat milk

4 shallots, sliced

10 black peppercorns

2 large tomatoes

40g salted butter

15g plain flour

1 teaspoon tomato paste

5 tablespoons finely sliced fresh basil

1 tablespoon freshly squeezed lemon juice

Salt and pepper

Unfortunately in Italy, turbot is not a fish that we eat often, but I had to include a recipe with it, because I think it's a fantastic fish. I created this beautiful cream of tomato to go with this dish, because the balance is just perfect and it brings the best out of the fish. Make sure you use freshly squeezed lemon juice for the sauce. You can substitute basil for parsley or 2 tablespoons of pesto. Perfect with Spicy Spinach with Garlic and Chillies (page 133).

For the sauce, put the milk in a small saucepan with the shallots and the peppercorns. Bring to the boil. Remove from the heat and leave to infuse for 15 minutes. Strain through a fine sieve.

In a second saucepan, dip the tomatoes into boiling water for 15 seconds, remove and peel off the skin. Cut in half, discard the seeds, slice into strips and set aside.

Melt 15g of the butter in a small saucepan, mix in the flour and, stirring with a wooden spoon, cook for about 1 minute. Remove from the heat and gradually stir in the infused milk. Season with salt. Bring the sauce to the boil, stirring constantly, then gently simmer for 2 minutes. Whisk in the tomato paste and basil and keep warm.

Preheat the grill. Melt the remaining butter and brush over both sides of the turbot. Grill for 5 minutes on each side.

Meanwhile, add the tomato strips to the sauce, along with the lemon juice. Stir and reheat gently.

To serve, place two turbot steaks on each plate and pour over the sauce.

Seared Tuna Steak with Courgettes and Capers

TONNO SCUE' SCUE'

Serves 4

100ml olive oil

4 tuna steaks (about 300g each)

3 garlic cloves, roughly sliced

5 tablespoons pine nuts

2 large courgettes, roughly sliced

200g cherry tomatoes, halved

5 tablespoons capers in salt, rinsed

1 tablespoon fresh thyme leaves, chopped

80g pitted green olives, halved

Salt and pepper

If you ever have the chance to visit the town where I was born, Torre del Greco, you will soon realise that every restaurant in town serves this dish. Southern Italian people, me included, are absolutely crazy about tuna. If you try to translate 'tonno scue' scue' into English, it would be 'tuna made with no effort'. The reason it is called this is because the few ingredients used are put together quite randomly with not much thought and yet the dish is still perfect with amazing flavours. Cooked in less than 15 minutes, it is something that I would definitely suggest after a long day.

Heat 5 tablespoons of the olive oil in a large frying pan and cook the tuna over a medium heat for 2 minutes on each side. Remove from the heat.

Heat the remaining oil in a second frying pan and fry the garlic, pine nuts and courgettes for 3–4 minutes over a high heat. Add in the cherry tomatoes, capers, thyme and olives and season with salt and pepper. Cook for a further minute.

Spoon the courgette mixture over the tuna and return the pan to a medium heat. Cook for a further 5 minutes, uncovered, to allow the fish to absorb the flavours.

To serve, place the tuna steaks in the centre of a serving plate and pour some of the courgette mixture over each portion.

Whole Baked Sea Bass Stuffed with Italian Salsa

Serves 4

4 whole sea bass (about 300g each)

6 unwaxed lemons

4 tablespoons finely chopped flat-leaf parsley

8 tablespoons extra virgin olive oil

4 tablespoons dry white wine

8 anchovy fillets in oil, drained and chopped

Salt and pepper

FOR THE SALSA

20 cherry tomatoes, quartered

1 red onion, finely chopped

200g roasted peppers from a jar, drained and chopped

100g pitted black olives, halved

10 tablespoons extra virgin olive oil

3 tablespoons white wine vinegar

This dish is definitely one of my top five signature dishes. I think I can comfortably say that I've shown how to make this dish in every cookery show I've appeared on. I strongly believe that this recipe is the best way to cook a whole fish. The only fiddly bit is boning the fish, but don't panic, have a look at the pictures and if you really feel worried, you can always ask your fishmonger to do it for you. (Please take my book with you, otherwise you may find it difficult to explain what you want). You can make this recipe by using a whole salmon, sea bream or a large trout.

To bone the fish (unless you can get your fishmonger to do it for you), place the whole fish on a chopping board, on its belly. Using a small sharp knife, cut down either side of the dorsal fin and along the backbone to free the two fillets from the central skeleton. Do not pierce the fish's belly. Work the backbone and ribs away from the flesh, from the head to within 2.5cm of its tail. Use kitchen scissors to sever the backbone at the head and tail. Gently pull out the backbone. Check for and remove any stray bones with your fingers.

Preheat the oven to 190°C/375°F/gas mark 5. Peel the lemons and chop up the skin. Mix the lemon skin in a large bowl with the parsley, olive oil, wine and anchovies. Season with salt and pepper. Mix well and spoon the mixture around the fish.

Slice the peeled lemons and spread to cover the bottom of a baking tray – this will prevent the fish from sticking to the tray and also infuse the fish with flavour. Place the prepared fish on top. Cook in the centre of the oven for about 20 minutes or until completely cooked.

Meanwhile, mix all the salsa ingredients together in a bowl and season.

Once the fish is cooked, use a tablespoon to gently remove the lemon mixture and discard.

Place the fish onto a serving plate and stuff with the Italian salsa. Serve immediately with a glass of dry Italian white wine.

I have to admit that I absolutely love meat. For me, it's the ultimate energy food. Whenever I feel down there is nothing that makes me happier than to have a really meaty dish; so much so that every time I do my tax return, my wife makes me a Polpettone alla Napoletana (page 104) that night.

I could easily write a thousand recipes about meat, but I have decided to go for my favourite regional dishes – with a Gino twist. The one I would choose for a dinner party is Rotolo di Maiale (page 103), because you can prepare it in advance, it's really easy to put together and it will look so good that your friends will think you are a genius.

Cooking tips

1. Do not overcook pork – it is safe to eat pork slightly more than medium
2. Ensure that chicken is always well cooked
3. To get the best flavour from beef, cook it medium or medium-rare
4. Do not season raw meat with salt as it will draw out the moisture from the meat
5. Good-quality meat from your butcher will make your dish taste ten times better
6. If you grill your meat, always make sure that the meat is at room temperature
7. If you are using a griddle pan, oil the meat not the pan, otherwise you will smoke out your kitchen. For beef and lamb, preheat the griddle pan until it is very hot, for pork it needs to be warm going on hot, so that the pork cooks through and is not pink
8. Never never never serve meat immediately after it's been cooked; always let it rest for at least one minute

Italian Shepherd's Pie

TORTA DEL PASTORE

Serves 6

5 tablespoons olive oil

1 large onion, finely chopped

3 carrots, chopped

70g button mushrooms, halved

500g minced beef

1 glass dry red wine

500g tinned chopped tomatoes

6 fresh basil leaves

700g sweet potatoes, chopped

30g salted butter

50ml full-fat milk

150g freshly grated Parmesan cheese

Salt and pepper

One of my favourite British dishes has to be shepherd's pie. You can't beat the combination of a perfectly textured mashed potato with a tasty meat sauce. Of course, like every great thing in life, you always try to improve it and I think with this dish, I've succeeded. My tip would be to use tinned chopped tomatoes, as their juice is thicker than the fresh ones, and plenty of fresh basil leaves – never use dry basil as it's horrible. You can bake this in a 2-litre pie dish or in smaller individual dishes.

Heat the olive oil in a large saucepan and fry the onion, carrots and mushrooms for 10 minutes until softened. Add the minced beef, season with salt and pepper and stir frequently with a wooden spoon for 5 minutes, separating any clumps of meat.

Add in the wine and simmer for about 10 minutes, stirring occasionally, until the alcohol has evaporated. Add the tomatoes and basil, taste for seasoning and cook, uncovered, over a medium heat for 30 minutes. Stir occasionally.

Meanwhile, preheat the oven to 200°C/400°F/gas mark 6. Cook the sweet potatoes in boiling salted water until soft. Drain and mash well, adding in the butter, milk and 100g of the Parmesan. Season with salt and pepper, then stir vigorously with a wooden spoon over a low heat for 2 minutes to give a creamy texture.

Pour the meat sauce into your pie dish(es) and carefully spread over the mashed potato, ensuring that the meat is completely covered. Use a fork to create small peaks and then sprinkle the remaining Parmesan on top. Bake in the centre of the oven for about 20 minutes or until the topping is crisp and golden. Serve immediately and enjoy with your friends.

Sirloin Steak in Pepper Crust with Peas

BISTECCA AL PEPE CON PISELLI

Serves 4

10 tablespoons olive oil

½ onion, finely chopped

2 celery sticks, finely chopped

1 medium carrot, finely chopped

400g frozen peas, thawed

200g tinned chopped tomatoes

100g toasted fine breadcrumbs
(see page 8)

70g black peppercorns, crushed

4 sirloin steaks

2 medium egg whites, lightly
beaten

Salt and pepper

I first read this recipe about ten years ago in an old Italian cookery book and once I saw the crusty steak served with the sweet peas, I couldn't resist trying it. I don't think I've altered the original recipe much and it definitely has to be one of my top 10 recipes that I've learned. If you fancy, you can always make it with a breast of chicken.

Heat 3 tablespoons of the olive oil in a frying pan and fry the onion until golden and soft. Add the celery and carrot and cook over a medium heat for 5 minutes until the vegetables soften. Add in the peas, stir well, and finally add in the chopped tomatoes. Season with salt and pepper and cook over a medium heat for about 10 minutes, stirring occasionally.

Meanwhile, mix together the breadcrumbs and crushed pepper in a bowl with a couple of pinches of salt. Dip the steaks into the egg white, then coat in the breadcrumb mixture.

Heat the remaining oil in a large frying pan and gently fry the steaks for about 2 minutes on each side until the coating is crisp and golden. Transfer to kitchen paper to allow any excess oil to drain.

To serve, place 3–4 tablespoons of the peas in the centre of each plate. Cut the steaks into thirds and place the pieces on top of the peas. Enjoy with a glass of dry Italian red wine.

Italian Sausage with Mushrooms and Cheesy Polenta

SALSICCE E POLENTA

Serves 4

6 tablespoons olive oil

1 large onion, finely sliced

6 Italian sausages with fennel, chopped into 2cm slices

100g chestnut mushrooms, sliced

100g oyster mushrooms, sliced

100g Porcini mushrooms, sliced

100g pitted Kalamata olives

200ml beef stock

Knob of butter

30g plain flour

400g quick-cook polenta

1 litre vegetable stock (or as much as your polenta packet recommends)

200g freshly grated Pecorino cheese

Salt and pepper

It is very traditional especially in northern Italy to serve sausages with polenta. A great dish to serve when you have loads of friends coming round, because you can serve it in the middle of the table and everybody can help themselves. If you can't find fresh Porcini mushrooms, use 15g of dried Porcini that has been soaked in 100ml of warm water together with 150g of flat mushrooms. Traditionally, this dish is always served on a wooden chopping board.

Heat the olive oil in a large saucepan and fry the onion, sausages and mushrooms over a medium heat for 8 minutes until golden, stirring occasionally. Add the olives, season with salt and pepper, add the beef stock and allow to simmer for about 10 minutes over a medium heat.

Dip the knob of butter into the plain flour, add to the sauce and stir, allowing the sauce to thicken very slowly.

Meanwhile, put the polenta and the vegetable stock into a medium saucepan and cook, stirring constantly with a wooden spoon, until it thickens. Add in the Pecorino, season with salt and pepper and stir well (the polenta should not be too hard; add some hot water, if necessary). Turn out onto a wooden board.

Spoon the sausages and sauce over the polenta and serve immediately on the board with a glass of dry Italian red wine.

Italian Lamb Casserole with Warm Salad

AGNELLO ALLA MENTA CON INSALATA CALDA

Serves 4

400g lamb steaks, cut into 2cm cubes

4 tablespoons finely chopped fresh rosemary

5 tablespoons finely chopped fresh mint

3 tablespoons white wine vinegar

3 tablespoons runny honey

5 tablespoons olive oil

2 large onions, finely chopped

100g button mushrooms

3 celery sticks, finely chopped

2 large potatoes, finely chopped

1 glass dry red wine

1 glass water

Salt and pepper

FOR THE WARM SALAD

5 tablespoons olive oil

3 courgettes, very finely sliced like matchsticks

2 carrots, very finely sliced like matchsticks

2 leeks, very finely sliced like matchsticks

6 tablespoons toasted pine nuts

Salt and pepper

After five years of cookery school and over ten years of experience, I have to admit that I never stop learning. I always think I know the best ways of cooking lamb and yet I am still finding better ways. This recipe came to me about five years ago when I started to appreciate the combination of mint with lamb after spending many years cooking lamb with rosemary. I can now say that I am absolutely addicted to this dish and recommend it to anyone who loves lamb casseroles. You can use neck of lamb instead of lamb steaks and my tip would be to rest the casserole for at least ten minutes before serving with the warm salad.

Put the lamb with the rosemary, mint, vinegar, honey, salt and pepper in a bowl. Cover with clingfilm and place in the fridge for about 4 hours to marinate.

Heat the olive oil in a large cast-iron casserole and fry the onions, mushrooms, celery and potatoes for about 5 minutes, stirring continuously with a wooden spoon. Add the lamb steaks along with the marinade, mix well and cook, uncovered, for a further 5 minutes, stirring.

Add the wine and cook for about 2 minutes to allow the alcohol to evaporate. Add the water, season with salt and pepper, cover the casserole with a lid and cook over a low heat for about 1½ hours, stirring occasionally.

Once the casserole is ready, prepare the salad. Heat the olive oil in a large frying pan and fry the sliced vegetables over a high heat for about 4 minutes, tossing continuously. Add the pine nuts and season with salt and pepper.

To serve, place some warm salad in the centre of each plate to form a nest and pour some of the lamb casserole in the middle.

Roast Pork Chops with Maple Syrup and Green Peppercorns

Serves 4

2 tablespoons whole green peppercorns

8 tablespoons maple syrup

4 tablespoons olive oil

1 tablespoon paprika

4 pork chops (about 250g each)

3 apples, peeled, cored and diced

2 tablespoons wholegrain mustard

300g spinach leaves

2 tablespoons extra virgin olive oil

2 tablespoons freshly squeezed lemon juice

Salt and pepper

I have to admit that I'm not a big fan of sweet and sour flavours, but since I've designed my own version, I am now converted of course. The combination of maple syrup with paprika is just perfect and with my fresh apple sauce added to the dish, it is beautiful. You can try this dish with chicken thighs – it would work just as well. My tip is to use firm apples and good-quality pork chops.

Mix together the peppercorns, maple syrup, half the olive oil and paprika in a large bowl. Place the chops in the bowl and leave to marinate in the fridge for at least 2 hours and for as long as possible.

Preheat the oven to 180°C/350°F/gas mark 4. Heat the remaining oil in an ovenproof frying pan and seal the pork for about 1 minute on each side. Use tongs to hold the chops and seal the fat on the side for about 1 minute. Pour the marinade over the chops and place the pan in the oven. Cook for about 15 minutes.

Meanwhile, put the apples in a small saucepan with 3 tablespoons of water and cook over a medium heat, stirring until they make a soft pulp. Remove from the heat and leave to cool slightly, then add the mustard and season with salt and pepper.

Cook the spinach in boiling salted water, drain thoroughly and place in a bowl. Dress with extra virgin olive oil and lemon juice, season with salt and mix well.

Place a pork chop in the centre of each plate, drizzle over the hot marinade, and serve with spinach and apple sauce on the side.

Baked Pork Tenderloin with Rosemary-flavoured Yorkshire Pudding

ROTOLO DI MAIALE

Serves 4

500g pork tenderloin

3 tablespoons finely chopped fresh rosemary

150g Parma ham, sliced

150g black olive paste or tapenade

1 medium egg, beaten in a bowl

Salt and pepper

FOR THE YORKSHIRE PUDDING

130g plain flour

2 tablespoons very finely chopped fresh rosemary

1 medium egg

200ml full-fat milk

100ml sparkling mineral water

10 tablespoons vegetable oil

FOR THE PASTRY

220g plain flour, plus extra for dusting

100g salted butter, chopped

This is one of my grandmother's special Sunday dishes – without the Yorkshire pudding of course. My sister Marcella and I were always very excited when we knew that Nonna Assunta was cooking this dish. The saltiness of the olive paste works absolutely fantastically with the sweetness of the pork and, of course, the crusty pastry around it makes it perfect. I created a rosemary-flavoured Yorkshire pudding to go with.

To make the pastry, mix the flour with a pinch of salt in a large bowl. Rub in the butter to create a breadcrumb texture. Add about 2 tablespoons of cold water to bind the pastry. Mix to a firm dough, wrap in clingfilm and leave to rest in the fridge for about 30 minutes.

Meanwhile, preheat the oven to 200°C/400°F/gas mark 6. Generously season the pork with salt, pepper and the rosemary. Wrap it in the Parma ham, ensuring the meat is completely covered.

Roll out the pastry on a well-floured surface until it makes a rectangle large enough to cover the meat. Gently spread over the black olive paste. Place the meat in the centre and wrap the pastry around it. Press the edges together to seal. Brush the top with the beaten egg, place on a baking tray and cook in the centre of the oven for about 40 minutes until golden.

Meanwhile, prepare the Yorkshire pudding. Mix together the flour, rosemary and egg with a pinch of salt in a large bowl. Add about half the milk and use a wooden spoon to gradually work it into the flour. Beat until the mixture is smooth, then add the remaining milk and the sparkling water. Continue to beat until well mixed and the surface is covered with little bubbles. Leave to rest for 20 minutes.

Pour the vegetable oil into a baking tray (or a 12-hole Yorkshire pudding tray) and place in the oven for 10 minutes until the oil is very hot. Pour the batter into the tray and cook for about 40 minutes until risen and golden brown.

When the pork is cooked, leave to rest for about 5 minutes. Slice and serve immediately with the rosemary Yorkshire pudding.

Neapolitan-style Meat Loaf

POLPETTONE ALLA NAPOLETANA

Serves 4

400g minced beef

400g minced pork

1 carrot, finely chopped

2 celery sticks, finely chopped

3 tablespoons chopped flat-leaf parsley

2 medium eggs

150g freshly grated Parmesan cheese

1 tablespoon extra virgin olive oil

50g bread, crusts removed and broken into small pieces

1 glass full-fat milk

4 boiled eggs, peeled

4 slices ham

1 glass dry white wine

Salt and pepper

If you go anywhere in Napoli, you will be served this traditional recipe. Great if you have a large family, it also can be eaten cold the day after you've made it. If you don't want to use pork, you can use minced lamb instead. Please make sure the meat loaf rests for at least five minutes before cutting it, so that you get the perfect slice.

Put the beef and pork mince, the carrot, celery, parsley, raw eggs, Parmesan and extra virgin olive oil in a large bowl. Season with salt and pepper and using your hands, mix well to combine all the ingredients.

Briefly soak the bread in the milk, drain and mix well with the meat mixture.

Cover the base of a baking tray with baking paper, place half of the meat mixture on the tray and flatten with your hands. Place the 4 hard-boiled eggs evenly down the centre of the mixture, then cover with the remaining meat. Use your hands to mould the meat loaf into an oval shape, cover with clingfilm and leave to rest in the fridge for 30 minutes before cooking. Meanwhile, preheat the oven to 160°C/325°F/gas mark 3.

Remove the loaf from the fridge, bring to room temperature and remove the clingfilm. Cook in the oven for about 1½ hours.

Twenty minutes before the end of the cooking, remove the loaf from the oven. Place the slices of ham over the loaf, pour the glass of white wine on top and return to the oven.

Leave the meat loaf to cool slightly before you slice it. Serve with a fresh salad of your choice.

Italian Chicken Curry

Serves 4

3 tablespoons olive oil

1 large onion, finely sliced

4 curry leaves

1.2kg skinless, boneless chicken breasts, cut into 3cm cubes

50ml double cream

100g sliced salame Milano, cut into strips

180ml coconut milk

Fresh coriander leaves, to garnish

Salt

FOR THE CURRY PASTE

3 green chillies, deseeded and chopped

½ teaspoon ground coriander

½ teaspoon turmeric

3 garlic cloves

1 teaspoon grated fresh ginger root

½ teaspoon ground cinnamon

2 tablespoons olive oil

My best friend Marco once told me that it is impossible for an Italian to create a curry. Of course, I had to prove him wrong, but in doing, I broke my cardinal rule and used onion and garlic together! I'm going to dedicate this recipe to all my Asian fans and to all curry lovers. Please let me know if you like it. You can substitute the salame Milano for cubed pancetta.

To make the paste, put the chillies, coriander, turmeric, garlic, ginger and cinnamon in a blender with the olive oil, 2 tablespoons of cold water and a couple of pinches of salt. Blitz to make a coarse paste.

Heat the olive oil in a large wok and fry the onion with the curry leaves over a medium heat for about 3 minutes until the onions have softened. Add the paste and cook for a further minute.

Add the chicken to the wok, mix well to coat with the sauce and cook for 5 minutes, stirring occasionally.

Add the cream, salame and coconut milk and cook, uncovered, over a medium heat for a further 8 minutes until the sauce starts to thicken.

Serve immediately, sprinkled with fresh coriander and your favourite fluffy rice.

Chicken Breasts in Lemon and Sage Sauce

POLLO AL LIMONE E SALVIA

Serves 4

2 tablespoons plain flour

Zest and juice of 1 unwaxed lemon

2 garlic cloves, crushed

4 skinless and boneless chicken breasts

3 tablespoons olive oil

1 teaspoon fennel seeds

300ml chicken stock

3 tablespoons freshly chopped sage

2 medium egg yolks

Sprigs of sage and slices of lemon

Salt and pepper

Every time my wife cooks for her girlfriends, she always makes this dish. I guess it's the freshness of the flavours and the simplicity of the cooking that works for her. Make sure once the dish is cooked, it's eaten straightaway, because as it cools down the chicken will dry. If you don't like fennel seeds, you can leave them out. Make sure the lemons are fresh and juicy.

In a small bowl, mix together the flour, lemon zest and garlic to create a paste. Lightly coat the chicken breasts with the lemon paste.

Preheat the oven to 180°C/350°F/gas mark 4. Remove the chicken from the paste, reserving the paste.

Heat the olive oil in a flameproof casserole and gently fry the chicken with the fennel seeds until lightly browned, turning once or twice.

With a wooden spoon, stir in any remaining lemon paste.

Add in the stock and sage and season with salt and pepper. Mix well and bring to the boil. Once it comes to the to boil, cover and bake in the oven for about 30 minutes.

In a bowl, mix together the egg yolks with 2 tablespoons of lemon juice.

Take the casserole dish out of the oven, stir the egg mixture into the casserole and put the dish back on the stove over a medium heat until the sauce thickens, stirring frequently. (Do not allow to boil.)

Once ready, adjust the seasoning and serve garnished with sage sprigs and lemon slices. Serve with your favourite rice.

Crispy Chicken Breasts Topped with Taleggio and Serrano Ham

POLLO IMPANATO ALLE NOCI CON SERRANO E TALEGGIO

Serves 4

100g toasted fine breadcrumbs (see page 8)

100g toasted mixed nuts, crushed

50g plain flour

2 medium eggs

1 tablespoon finely chopped flat-leaf parsley

4 skinless, boneless chicken breasts

10 tablespoons olive oil

300g Taleggio cheese

8 slices Serrano ham

Salt and pepper

FOR THE SAUCE

5 tablespoons olive oil

1 large red onion, finely sliced

8 anchovy fillets in oil, drained

800g tinned cherry tomatoes

2 tablespoons finely chopped flat-leaf parsley

The worse thing you can do to a chicken breast is of course to overcook it and dry it out. The idea for this recipe came from a northern Italian dish called Vitello alla Milanese (Veal Milanese) and my twist is mixing the breadcrumbs with crushed nuts. This dish combines the crunchiness of the coating, the ooziness of the cheese and the saltiness of the ham – it would be impossible not to like it. Served with a cherry tomato sauce, it is colourful and full of flavour. You can adapt my recipe with any melting cheese and substitute the Serrano ham for any cured ham.

To prepare the sauce, heat the olive oil in a medium saucepan and fry the onion and anchovies for 6 minutes until golden. Add in the cherry tomatoes and parsley, season with salt and pepper and cook, uncovered, over a medium heat for about 10 minutes, stirring occasionally with a wooden spoon.

Meanwhile, preheat the grill. Mix together the breadcrumbs, nuts and flour on a large plate. Gently beat the eggs with the parsley and a pinch of seasoning in a large bowl.

With a meat mallet, beat the chicken breasts between two sheets of clingfilm on a board until the breasts are 1cm thin. Dip into the eggs, then coat in the breadcrumb mixture.

Heat the olive oil in a large frying pan and gently fry the chicken for about 4 minutes on each side until crisp and golden. Transfer to kitchen paper to allow any excess oil to drain.

Put the chicken on a baking tray and top each one with two slices of Taleggio. Place under a hot grill until the cheese has melted.

To serve, spread 4–5 tablespoons of the sauce in the centre of each plate and place a chicken breast on top. Gently arrange two slices of Serrano ham in folds over the melted cheese and serve immediately, accompanied by a glass of dry Italian white wine.

VEG OUT

I thought I would find this chapter very hard to write, simply because I love meat and fish and I often eat vegetarian dishes as a side dish. Luckily, a lot of Italian recipes are vegetarian so when I started writing, it proved to be easier than I had anticipated. Take pasta for example, I strongly believe that it's probably the most versatile vegetarian dish that you will ever find.

Most of the recipes that I have chosen are from southern Italy and are made with easy, accessible ingredients.

Cooking tips

1. Make sure you choose vegetables that are in season and if the ones I've used in my recipes aren't in season, experiment with alternatives
2. Veggie dishes are the ultimate quick meals, as they don't need much cooking
3. I can't stress enough how important it is not to overcook veg – not only will you lose their vibrant colour, but you will also lose their nutrients
4. If you fancy the Italian Shepherd's Pie (page 96), you can easily replace the minced beef with minced quorn
5. Try the Melanzane alla Parmigiana (page 30) – it will also make a fantastic main course

Italian-style Spring Rolls

BOMBE DI VERDURE

Serves 4

4 tablespoons olive oil

1 red pepper, deseeded and finely sliced

1 courgette, finely sliced like matchsticks

1 carrot, finely sliced like matchsticks

1 leek, finely sliced like matchsticks

150g button mushrooms, sliced

2 garlic cloves, finely chopped

½ teaspoon crushed dry chillies

16 sheets filo pastry (15 x 15cm)

100g melted butter

Salt and pepper

One of my favourite oriental dishes has to be vegetable spring rolls and I make it so often at home that I had to include it in my book. It's a fantastic dish to prepare when you have parties, because you can fry them in the afternoon and then reheat them in the oven ready for your guests. Ensure the vegetables are not too wet when putting them into the filo pastry, otherwise your spring rolls will go soggy. If you don't have one of the vegetables, don't panic — you can always do without. Please don't try to make fresh filo pastry, the ready-made type is perfectly fine.

Heat the olive oil in a wok or large frying pan and fry all the vegetables, the garlic and the chilli over a high heat, uncovered, for 15 minutes. Stir continuously and season with salt. Once all the vegetables are golden and soft, remove using a slotted spoon and leave to cool.

Preheat the oven to 180°C/350°F/gas mark 4. Brush all the filo pastry sheets with the melted butter and stick them together in twos to make eight strong ones. Brush these eight sheets with more melted butter and share out the cooled vegetables between them, placing them diagonally across each sheet. Start to roll one corner of the filo towards the middle. When you reach the centre, tuck in the sides to encase the filling, then continue to roll up, creating a large roll.

Place the prepared rolls on a greased baking tray and brush them with the remaining melted butter. Sprinkle with black pepper.

Bake in the oven for about 15 minutes or until browned and crispy. Serve immediately with sweet chilli sauce.

Spinach, Ricotta and Goat's Cheese Terrine

SFORMATO DI SPINACI

114

Serves 4

2 tablespoons olive oil, plus extra for greasing

3 spring onions, finely chopped

230g spinach leaves, chopped

200g ricotta cheese

150g goat's cheese

3 medium eggs

280ml double cream

100g shelled, toasted walnuts, to garnish

Salt and pepper

This recipe is probably one of my favourite ways to use goat's cheese. The balance of flavours between spinach, goat's cheese and toasted walnuts works beautifully. It is a great dish that can be served as a starter or main course. You can use rocket leaves instead of spinach if you prefer, and make sure that you serve my terrine with plenty of warm crusty bread – see page 137 for my bread recipe.

Lightly oil a 1.4-litre ovenproof terrine dish and line the base and sides with non-stick baking paper. Lightly brush with oil again.

Heat the olive oil in a large frying pan and gently fry the spring onions for 2 minutes. Add in the spinach, season with salt and pepper and cook over a medium heat until the spinach has wilted and all excess liquid has evaporated. Remove the pan from the heat and leave to cool.

Preheat the oven to 180°C/350°F/gas mark 4. Transfer the spinach mixture to a food-processor with the cheeses, eggs and double cream. Season with salt and pepper and blend until smooth.

Pour the mixture into the terrine and cover with a piece of oiled foil. Place the terrine in a deep-sided baking tray and pour in enough hot water to come halfway up the sides of the terrine.

Cook in the oven for about 2 hours or until a skewer inserted into the centre of the terrine comes out clean. Remove from the oven and leave to cool. When completely cold, pour off any excess liquid from the terrine and chill in the fridge for 2 hours.

Turn out the terrine onto a serving plate and cut into thick slices. Garnish with the walnuts and serve with toasted bread.

VEG OUT

Asparagus and Gorgonzola Soufflé

Serves 2

350g trimmed asparagus spears

50g salted butter, plus extra for greasing

3 tablespoons plain flour

200ml full-fat milk

4 medium eggs, separated

120g Gorgonzola cheese

Salt and pepper

Many people think that you need to be a chef to make a soufflé, but I completely disagree. My friends have tried this recipe many times and every time they have come back to me saying that it is one of the easiest soufflés that they have ever made. Of course, the combination of the Gorgonzola cheese with the asparagus is amazing, but if you want to make it when asparagus is not in season, you can always use courgettes. This recipe will make everybody believe that you are a professional, because not only does it taste fantastic, but it also looks elegant and beautiful. Whenever you make a soufflé, make sure that you bake it in the middle of the oven to avoid burning the top.

Cook the asparagus in boiling salted water until soft. Drain, allow to cool and finely chop.

Preheat the oven to 180°C/350°F/gas mark 4. Grease a soufflé dish (about 1.3 litres).

Melt the butter in a medium saucepan, add in the asparagus and cook for about 2 minutes, allowing any excess moisture to evaporate. Mix in the flour and cook very gently for a further minute. Stir in the milk, season with salt and pepper and bring to the boil slowly. Reduce the heat and keep stirring with a wooden spoon until it thickens.

Cool slightly, then beat in the egg yolks a little at a time and half the Gorgonzola.

Whisk the egg whites in a large clean bowl until stiff and fold into the mixture.

Transfer the mixture to the soufflé dish and sprinkle with the remaining Gorgonzola. Bake in the centre of the oven for about 30 minutes until well risen. Serve immediately with your favourite salad.

Italian Fondue

FONDUTA DI FORMAGGI

Serves 4

1 garlic clove

3 tablespoons Kirsch

2 teaspoons cornflour

200g Emmental cheese, grated

100g Taleggio cheese, cut into small cubes

50g Gorgonzola cheese, cut into small cubes

100g Gruyère cheese, grated

220ml dry white wine

1 focaccia loaf, sliced

Paprika

Salt and pepper

This is what I call a fun dish, the kind of dish I like to do when I want something tasty, quick and with hardly any effort. The combination of the bread dipped in melted cheese is the ultimate taste experience. I remember very clearly that this used to be one of my grandmother's favourite dishes — she loved any kind of fondue. You can substitute the chunks of bread for chunks of celery, carrots or yellow peppers. If you find the Gorgonzola cheese too strong, use Dolcelatte.

Rub the garlic around the inside of a heavy-based saucepan or a fondue pan.

Whisk the Kirsch with the cornflour in a small bowl to make a smooth paste.

Put the four cheeses in the pan with the wine and the cornflour paste and gently bring to the boil, uncovered, stirring frequently with a wooden spoon. As soon as it starts to boil, reduce the heat and simmer for 3 minutes, stirring frequently. Season with salt and pepper (go easy with the salt, because the cheeses are salty).

Meanwhile, toast the focaccia slices and cut into bite-sized chunks. Once ready, set the pan over a fondue burner, sprinkle with paprika and bring to the table to share with your friends.

(If you don't have a fondue set, transfer the fondue to a warmed serving dish and keep warm over a heated serving tray.)

Cannelloni with Courgettes, Rocket and Mascarpone

CANNELLONI AL FORNO

Serves 4

4 tablespoons olive oil, plus extra for greasing

2 large courgettes, cut into small cubes

400g rocket leaves, roughly chopped

450g mascarpone cheese

1 teaspoon grated nutmeg

200g freshly grated Parmesan cheese

1kg tinned chopped tomatoes

5 tablespoons extra virgin olive oil

10 fresh basil leaves

16 sheets fresh lasagne or ready-rolled dried cannelloni tubes

100ml double cream

Salt and pepper

Cannelloni is what I call a traditional Italian recipe, and it is usually filled with ricotta and spinach. My twist on this Italian classic is to use rocket leaves and mascarpone cheese. Believe me, if you make them my way, they will be lighter and yet still full of flavour. Make sure that you rest this pasta dish for at least five minutes before serving, allowing all the flavours to marry together.

Heat the olive oil in a large frying pan and fry the courgettes and rocket leaves over a medium heat for 8 minutes or until soft. Season with salt and pepper and set aside to cool.

Preheat the oven to 200°C/400°F/gas mark 6. Mix the mascarpone with the courgettes and rocket in a large bowl. Add in the nutmeg and half the Parmesan. Season with salt and pepper and mix well.

Tip the chopped tomatoes into another large bowl, season with salt and pepper, and stir in the extra virgin olive oil and basil.

Lay the lasagne sheets on the work surface and divide the mascarpone mixture between them. Roll up the sheets to secure the filling. Place the prepared cannelloni, seam-side down, in a single layer in a greased baking dish measuring 25 x 30cm. Pour over the tomatoes and drizzle the double cream on top.

Bake in the centre of the oven for 15 minutes, then sprinkle with the remaining Parmesan and return to the oven for a further 15 minutes.

Remove from the oven, leave to rest for 5 minutes, then serve.

Potato Dumplings with Tomato and Basil Sauce

Serves 4

1kg floury potatoes (King Edward or Maris Piper), unpeeled

2 medium eggs, beaten

300g plain flour, plus extra for dusting

FOR THE SAUCE

4 tablespoons olive oil

1 medium onion, finely chopped

700g passata (sieved tomatoes)

10 fresh basil leaves

100g freshly grated Parmesan cheese

Salt and white pepper

If I had to choose one recipe that gives me the greatest pleasure to cook with my children, it would have to be this one! It's probably the only time that I don't mind making a mess in the kitchen. Gnocchi has such a unique flavour that I don't think it should ever be served with anything but a simple tomato and basil sauce. Always ensure you serve it with plenty of freshly grated Parmesan cheese on top and, if you make it for a large number of people, place in a baking tray with the tomato sauce, sprinkle over the cheese and bake in the oven at 220°C/425°F/gas mark 7 for 10 minutes.

Place the potatoes in a large saucepan, cover with salted water and bring to the boil. Cook for 15–20 minutes until tender and drain.

Peel the hot potatoes and tip into a large bowl. Mash quickly, then stir in the eggs and flour while the mash is still hot. Season with salt and pepper.

Use your hands to work the mixture on a floured surface for about 3 minutes to create a soft dough texture. Take a handful of the potato mixture and roll into a long thin sausage shape about 1.5cm thick. Cut into pieces, each about 1.5cm long. Continue in this way until all the potato mixture has been turned into small dumplings.

With your thumb roll each gnocchi against a fork to form ridges on one side. Place the gnocchi on a well-floured tray and set aside.

To prepare the sauce, heat the olive oil in a large frying pan and fry the onion over a medium heat for 8 minutes or until golden. Add the passata and the basil, season with salt and pepper and cook, uncovered, over a low heat for about 10 minutes.

Bring a large saucepan of salted water to the boil. Cook the gnocchi, in batches if necessary, by lowering them into the water. As soon as they rise to the surface, use a wire scoop to transfer them to the pan with the tomato sauce. Gently stir the gnocchi into the sauce and cook over a low heat for a further 2 minutes. Serve immediately, sprinkled with plenty of Parmesan.

Baked Aubergines with Spinach and Pecorino

Serves 4

2 aubergines (about 200g each)

4 tablespoons olive oil, plus extra for greasing

150g frozen spinach, thawed and chopped

3 tablespoons chopped flat-leaf parsley

80g freshly grated Pecorino cheese

5 tablespoons toasted pine nuts

400g tinned chopped tomatoes

2 Mozzarella balls, drained and sliced

1 ciabatta loaf, cut into 2cm slices

2 garlic cloves

Salt and pepper

I learnt this recipe in a restaurant in Roma as I was filming 'La Prova del Cuoco', an Italian cookery show. I remember how as I was eating, it I felt such an explosion of flavours and texture in my mouth. Of course, I had to have a chat with the chef and he told me that this dish was the most popular in the restaurant. I managed to convince him to give me his secret recipe and after adding a few of my touches, I think I've probably got the best aubergine recipe. Ensure your aubergines are nice and fat, as you will need plenty of space for filling them. You can substitute pine nuts for walnuts or pistachio nuts and if you don't want to use Mozzarella, you can use any melting cheese.

Preheat the oven to 180°C/350°F/gas mark 4.

Halve the aubergines lengthways and place on a greased baking tray, skin-side down. Score the flesh with a sharp knife and bake in the oven for 25 minutes. Remove from the oven and set aside to cool.

Use a tablespoon to gently scoop out the flesh of the aubergines, keeping the skin intact. Place the flesh on a board, roughly chop, then transfer to a large bowl. Add in the spinach, parsley, Pecorino cheese, pine nuts and chopped tomatoes. Season with salt and pepper, 2 tablespoons of the olive oil and mix well.

Use the mixture to fill the cavity in the reserved aubergine skins, then return to the baking tray skin-side down. Lay the Mozzarella slices on top, drizzle with the remaining olive oil and return to the oven and bake for about 15 minutes until they are golden and the cheese has melted.

Meanwhile, toast the ciabatta, then rub the garlic all over the slices.

Once the aubergines are cooked, leave to rest for 2 minutes and serve with the warm garlic ciabatta.

Moroccan-style Pasta

PAPPARDELLE ALLA MAROCCHINA

Serves 4

6 tablespoons olive oil

1 onion, finely sliced

8 medium tomatoes, chopped, skin and seeds included

1 teaspoon ground cinnamon

1 teaspoon ground cumin

120g tinned chickpeas, drained

120g flaked almonds, toasted

500g pappardelle

3 tablespoons chopped flat-leaf parsley

2 tablespoons chopped fresh coriander

Salt and pepper

In the summer of 1995, I was working as a head chef in the famous Mambo King restaurant in Puerto Banus when I met a great Moroccan chef who also knew a lot about Italian cuisine. I can clearly remember his versions of many Italian classic dishes such as pastas, stews and even desserts, but the one that stood out was this dish. Even today, I still find its combination of flavours and spices really appealing. The greatest thing about this recipe is that you can use any shape of pasta that you fancy, and if you don't want to use coriander, you can use chopped parsley. Reserve a few herbs and flaked almonds to garnish the finished dish.

Heat the olive oil in a large frying pan and fry the onion for about 8 minutes until soft and light brown. Add in the tomatoes and spices and cook, uncovered, over a medium heat for 15 minutes until the tomatoes break down. Stir occasionally. Season with salt and pepper, add in the chickpeas and almonds and cook for a further 5 minutes.

Meanwhile, cook the pasta in a large pan of boiling salted water until al dente. Drain and add to the frying pan. Stir the pasta into the sauce over a medium heat for 1 minute, then add the herbs and continue to stir for a further minute. Serve immediately with a cold beer.

Italian Tortilla with Peppers and Parmesan

TORTILLA ALL'ITALIANA

Serves 4

10 tablespoons olive oil

250g onions, thinly sliced

650g baking potatoes, peeled

2 red peppers, deseeded and sliced

6 medium eggs

3 tablespoons chopped flat-leaf parsley

50g freshly shaved Parmesan cheese

Salt and pepper

If you want to cook something that you can eat the same night and then again for lunch the next day, this is definitely the one you should try. I love these kinds of recipes, where all the ingredients used are mainly simple ingredients that you would probably find lying around in your kitchen. A great dish if you don't want to do a lot of washing up and, served with a nice salad, it becomes an extremely satisfying and comforting meal. Try to avoid using green peppers for this recipe, as they are very bitter and you can easily substitute Parmesan cheese for Cheddar cheese.

Heat 5 tablespoons of the olive oil in a large frying pan and gently fry the onions over a medium heat for about 10 minutes or until golden and softened.

Meanwhile, thinly slice the potatoes (use a mandolin, if possible), then add to the onion together with the peppers and cook for a further 10 minutes, stirring frequently. Leave to cool and transfer to a large bowl.

Whisk the eggs with the parsley in a separate bowl, season with salt and pepper and add to the bowl with the potatoes. Mix well to combine and leave to rest for 2 minutes.

Meanwhile, preheat the grill. Use some kitchen paper to clean the frying pan and heat the remaining olive oil. Add the potato mixture to the hot frying pan, pressing it down gently. Cook, uncovered, over a medium heat for 8 minutes or until the base is golden brown.

Sprinkle the top with the Parmesan and place under the hot grill for about 4 minutes until the top sets and the cheese crisps up. (Remember to protect the pan handle with foil if necessary.)

Enjoy the tortilla either warm or cold with your favourite salad.

Sour Cream Potato Bake with Aubergines and Taleggio

Serves 4

5 tablespoons olive oil

300g aubergines, cut into 2cm cubes

650g onions, finely sliced

1 tablespoon soft brown sugar

950g Jersey royal potatoes, peeled

220g sour cream

1 tablespoon finely chopped thyme

Butter, for greasing

250g Taleggio cheese, chopped into small pieces

300ml vegetable stock

Salt and white pepper

If I ever decide to become a vegetarian, I would definitely choose this recipe as one of my regular dishes. This recipe was really a mistake, that came together when I threw together everything I had in the cupboard and fridge. Believe me when I say that this is probably the best mistake I have ever made. I've tried Cheddar cheese instead of Taleggio and it still works beautifully. A great dish to prepare in the afternoon, ready to be baked later the same evening.

Heat the olive oil in a large frying pan and fry the aubergines over a medium heat for about 15 minutes until golden and crispy. Transfer using a slotted spoon to a plate.

Reduce the heat to moderate and cook the onions with the sugar in the frying pan for about 20 minutes until soft and caramelised. Stir occasionally.

Meanwhile, put the potatoes in a large saucepan and cover with cold salted water. Bring to the boil, cook for about 10 minutes, then drain. Preheat the oven to 220°C/425°F/gas mark 7.

Once the potatoes are cool enough to handle, cut into 1cm-thick slices. Place in a large bowl and gently mix with the sour cream and thyme. Season with salt and pepper.

Butter a shallow 2-litre ovenproof dish and cover the base with half the potatoes. Sprinkle with the onions, aubergines and two thirds of the chopped Taleggio.

Cover evenly with the remaining potatoes and pour over the vegetable stock. Sprinkle the remaining cheese on top and cook in the centre of the oven for about 40 minutes or until golden brown. Remove from the oven and leave to rest for 5 minutes.

Serve immediately with a crisp green salad.

A good side dish is a crucial part of your main course, but it is often treated with not as much respect as it deserves. I feel that the selection I have chosen is a good balance for the main courses featured in this book. Many of these recipes can also be used as a vegetarian option – for example, the Peperonata (page 131).

The secret of choosing a good side dish is simple – you need to try to complement the flavour. For instance, if you have a very delicate fish course, do not choose a side dish that will overpower the flavour of the fish – my recommendation for fish would be something as simple as Spinaci all'Arrabbiata (page 133).

Cooking tips

1. Do not choose a cheesy side dish if you are having fish
2. Do not choose a fishy side dish if you are having meat
3. Always try to make at least two side dishes
4. Never serve your side dish on the same plate as your main course (I don't think the flavours should be mixed on the same plate)
5. Try to have a good balance of colour between a side dish and the main course
6. Make your own bread such as the Schiacciata Toscana (page 137) and I guarantee that your guests will be impressed
7. To make a mash with a lovely texture and without any lumps, use a potato ricer, which looks like a large garlic crusher, instead of a masher.

Celery Gratin

SEDANI GRATINATI

Serves 6

2 heads celery

3 bay leaves

250g sour cream

1 teaspoon paprika

3 tablespoons chopped flat-leaf parsley

60g toasted fine breadcrumbs (see page 8)

60g freshly grated Parmesan cheese

Salt

Celery is unfortunately not a vegetable that many people would choose to use as a side dish. To me, this is a great shame because, cooked in the right way, it makes a great side dish to accompany most meals but especially meat. Because I've used Parmesan cheese for this dish, try to avoid serving it with fish – remember my rule is never serve fish with cheese. You can replace the parsley with chives or fresh basil and the sour cream with crème fraîche.

Preheat the oven to 200°C/400°F/gas mark 6. Trim the celery, discarding any tough outer stalks and cut into 6cm lengths. Reserve all the inner leaves.

Bring a large saucepan of salted water to the boil and cook the celery with the bay leaves for 8 minutes until al dente. Drain, discard the bay leaves and transfer to a gratin dish.

Finely chop the reserved celery leaves and place in a large bowl. Add the sour cream, the paprika and parsley, season with salt and mix well.

Pour the cream mixture over the celery, sprinkle with the breadcrumbs and Parmesan and bake in the oven for about 30 minutes or until the top is crisp and golden brown.

Cauliflower with Capers and Olives

CAVOLFIORE ALLA CONTADINA

Serves 6

500g cauliflower, cut into florets

4 tablespoons extra virgin olive oil

2 garlic cloves, finely sliced

60g anchovy fillets in olive oil

2 tablespoons capers in salt, rinsed

40g pitted Kalamata olives, chopped

3 tablespoons chopped flat-leaf parsley

Salt

It wasn't until I came to England that I came across cauliflower regularly. For me, it can be a little bland, so here I've added some stronger flavours.

Bring a large saucepan of salted water to the boil and cook the cauliflower for 6 minutes until al dente.

Meanwhile, heat the oil in a small saucepan and gently fry the garlic and anchovies over a medium heat for 1 minute, stirring frequently. Add the capers, olives and parsley, mix and transfer to a large bowl.

Drain the cauliflower and place in the bowl with the garlic and anchovy mixture. Toss gently to avoid breaking up the cauliflower.

Serve hot as an accompaniment to fish or meat – it's good with lamb.

Roasted Peppers with Olives, Capers and Garlic

PEPERONATA

Serves 6

2 whole green peppers

2 whole red peppers

2 whole yellow peppers

3 tablespoons olive oil

1 garlic clove, finely sliced

1 tablespoon capers in salt, rinsed

100g pitted Kalamata olives

1 tablespoon chopped flat-leaf parsley

Salt and pepper

This is a recipe that comes from the mountains of Avellino, a town near Napoli where they are mad about roasted peppers.

Preheat the oven to 200°C/400°F/gas mark 6. Place the peppers on a baking tray and roast for about 20 minutes. Transfer the hot peppers to a large bowl, cover with clingfilm and leave to cool. Once cooled, peel off the skin, halve the peppers lengthways and discard the seeds and stalks. Cut into 1 cm slices. Set aside on a chopping board.

Heat the olive oil in a medium saucepan and fry the garlic over a medium heat until golden. Add in the peppers, capers and olives. Season with salt and pepper and add the parsley. Mix well and cook, uncovered, over a low heat for 20 minutes, stirring occasionally.

Serve hot with your favourite fish or meat dish, or cold on top of some crusty bread or bruschetta.

Roast Potatoes with Garlic and Rosemary

Serves 4

1kg small floury potatoes, unpeeled

6 tablespoons olive oil

1 tablespoon walnut oil

15 garlic cloves, unpeeled

5 tablespoons fresh rosemary, stripped from stalks

Sea salt and pepper

Whenever I cook a roast dinner at home, this is the dish I choose to accompany it. I strongly believe that there is nothing better than garlic and fresh rosemary with a good roast potato, and the touch of walnut oil makes it perfect.

Put the potatoes in a large saucepan, cover with cold water and bring to the boil. Cook for 3 minutes and drain.

Preheat the oven to 200°C/400°F/gas mark 6. Pour both oils into a roasting tin and place in the oven to get really hot.

Tip the potatoes into the hot oil with the garlic and rosemary. Season, mix well and roast in the oven for 35–40 minutes, basting occasionally. Serve with a few cloves of roasted garlic on each portion.

Spicy Spinach with Garlic and Chillies

Serves 6

6 tablespoons olive oil

2 garlic cloves, finely sliced

2 small red chillies, deseeded and finely sliced

500g spinach, drained

Freshly squeezed lemon juice

Salt

I have to agree with Popeye; there is nothing healthier or tastier than a good plate of spinach. The combination of the garlic and the chilli works beautifully with the sweetness of the spinach and, of course not only do you need one saucepan to cook it, but it only takes a few minutes to prepare.

Heat the olive oil in a large saucepan and fry the garlic and chillies over a medium heat for 1 minute. Add the spinach, season with salt and mix.

Continue to cook, uncovered, over a medium heat for about 10 minutes until all the water from the spinach has evaporated, stirring occasionally.

Serve hot or cold with a squeeze of lemon juice.

Italian-style Broccoli Stir-fry

BROCCOLI SALTATI

Serves 6

5 tablespoons olive oil

2 tablespoons runny honey

1 tablespoon light soy sauce

2 tablespoons balsamic vinegar

1 garlic clove, finely sliced

1 small red chilli, deseeded and finely sliced

3 tablespoons sliced fresh basil leaves

60g pine nuts

700g broccoli, cut into florets

Salt and pepper

Everybody in my family loves broccoli and we always have it in the house. One day I thought I would experiment with a few oriental ingredients. This is what came out of that day and I must say that I was so excited about the flavours that I decided to put it in this book.

Mix together 1 tablespoon of the olive oil, the honey, soy sauce, balsamic vinegar, garlic, chilli, basil and pine nuts in a large bowl.

Bring a large saucepan of salted water to the boil and cook the broccoli for 3 minutes until al dente. Drain the broccoli and place in the bowl with the dressing. Toss gently to avoid breaking up the broccoli.

Heat the remaining olive oil in a wok and fry the broccoli with the dressing for 4 minutes until piping hot, stirring frequently.

Check the seasoning and serve hot as an accompaniment to fish or meat.

The Ultimate Cheesy Mash

PURÉ DI PATATE

Serves 4

1kg potatoes (King Edward are best), peeled

150ml full-fat milk

100g freshly grated Parmesan cheese

50g freshly grated Cheddar cheese

100g salted butter

Salt and white pepper

There is nothing I hate more than a boring, tasteless, lumpy mash. This side dish goes perfectly with any kind of meat, especially with sausages and steak.

Put the potatoes in a large saucepan, cover with cold water and bring to the boil. Cook until tender. Drain and mash in the saucepan.

Return the pan to a low heat and use a wooden spoon to stir in the milk and beat to a creamy texture. Add in the cheeses, the butter, season with salt and pepper and continue to stir for a further 3 minutes over a low heat until the cheeses are completely melted. Serve immediately.

Deep-fried Polenta with Sage and Pancetta

POLENTA FRITTA CON PANCETTA

Serves 4

300g quick-cook polenta

5 tablespoons olive oil

2 onions, finely sliced

6 sage leaves, finely sliced

100g pancetta, finely diced

100g freshly grated Pecorino cheese

1 litre oil for frying, e.g. vegetable or sunflower oil

Butter, for greasing

Salt and pepper

If you like chunky chips, try this. It goes well with fish and meat, and if you make a big batch, you can reheat in the oven.

Bring a saucepan of salted water to the boil and cook the polenta until it thickens (follow the instructions on the packet).

Meanwhile, heat the olive oil in a medium frying pan and fry the onions, sage and the pancetta for 8 minutes until golden, stirring frequently.

Add the onion mixture to the polenta, along with the Pecorino. Season with salt and pepper and mix well using a wooden spoon.

Pour the mixture into a buttered dish about 20cm square and 3cm deep and leave to cool.

Once cooled and firm, tip the polenta onto a chopping board. Cut into slices about the size of a fish finger and deep-fry in hot oil for about 1 minute until crisp and golden. Drain on kitchen paper and serve.

Baked Polenta Topped with Four Cheeses

POLENTA AI QUATTRO FORMAGGI

Serves 4

300g quick-cook polenta

Butter, for greasing

4 large plum tomatoes, sliced

100g Gorgonzola cheese, 100g Taleggio cheese, 100g strong Cheddar cheese, all at room temperature

100g grated Parmesan cheese

Salt and pepper

This is a northern Italian recipe which I came across when I was working in Bologna, and it is a brilliant alternative to potatoes or rice.

Bring a saucepan of salted water to the boil and cook the polenta until it thickens (follow the instructions on the packet). Season and pour the mixture into a buttered dish about 20 x 25cm and leave to cool.

Meanwhile, preheat the oven to 180°C/350°F/gas mark 4. Once the polenta is cooled and firm, place the tomatoes on top. Break the Gorgonzola, Taleggio and Cheddar into small pieces into a large bowl. Mix together, add the Parmesan and continue to mix. Sprinkle over the tomatoes. Bake in the centre of the oven for about 8 minutes until the cheeses are melted and lightly browned.

Tuscan-style Bread with Rosemary and Extra Virgin Olive Oil

SCHIACCIATA TOSCANA

Serves 4

450g strong plain white flour, plus extra for dusting

1 teaspoon fast-action dried yeast

130ml extra virgin olive oil, plus extra for greasing

2 tablespoons fresh rosemary, stripped from stalks

Coarse sea salt, for sprinkling

No Italian meal would be authentic if it wasn't served with a good-quality bread. Personally, I would not be able to eat any starter or main course if not accompanied with some kind of bread on the side. I chose this bread, because it is easy to make and it goes well with any kind of dish. Of course, I don't suggest that you should bake your own bread all the time, but I do believe everybody should experience the satisfaction of doing so if only once. Make sure that you always, always use fresh rosemary because the flavour is much better and, of course, a good-quality extra virgin olive oil, preferably Italian – the smell and the colour is just fantastico.

Mix together the flour and yeast in a large bowl. Make a well in the centre and pour in 300ml of warm water with 6 tablespoons of the olive oil. Mix well to make a soft dough.

Turn out the dough onto a floured surface and knead for 10 minutes until smooth and elastic. Place in an oiled bowl, cover with a tea-towel and leave in a warm place to rise for 1 hour until it has doubled in size.

Turn out onto a floured surface again and knead the dough for a further 2 minutes, then roll out to a large rectangle about 2cm thick.

Transfer the dough onto an oiled baking tray, cover with oiled clingfilm and leave to rise again for about 25 minutes. Meanwhile, preheat the oven to 220°/425°F/gas mark 7.

Remove the clingfilm and prick the risen dough all over with a fork. Brush the dough with half the remaining oil and sprinkle with the rosemary and sea salt.

Bake in the centre of the oven for 30–35 minutes until golden and brown. Remove from the baking tray and transfer to a wire rack. As it cools, brush with the remaining oil to soften the crust.

Potatoes, Peppers and Shallots Roasted with Rosemary and Thyme

PATATE ALL'ORTOLANA

Serves 4

600g small floury potatoes, unpeeled

8 tablespoons olive oil

2 sweet yellow peppers

15 shallots

2 thyme sprigs

3 tablespoons fresh rosemary, stripped from stalks

15 cherry tomatoes, on the vine

Sea salt and pepper

Whenever my mother had guests over for dinner, this would be the recipe she would choose to accompany the main meal. I remember my sister and I used to love it when we knew this was on the menu and always begged her to make twice as much. The combination of the roasted peppers with the shallots and the fresh cherry tomatoes is an unbelievable experience that everybody should try. You can substitute yellow peppers with green peppers, and if you don't have shallots, you can use a normal white onion.

Put the potatoes in a large saucepan, cover with cold water and bring to the boil. Cook for 3 minutes and drain.

Preheat the oven to 200°C/400°F/gas mark 6. Pour the oil into a large roasting tin and place in the oven to get really hot.

Meanwhile, trim and deseed the peppers and cut into large chunks. Peel the shallots, allowing them to fall into their natural segments.

Once the vegetables are prepared, tip into the hot oil with the thyme and rosemary. Season with salt and pepper, mix well and roast for 30 minutes, basting occasionally.

Add the cherry tomatoes, roast for a further 10 minutes, and serve immediately.

A BIT ON THE SIDE

I think that a good meal should always be followed by a good dessert. The ones I have chosen for this chapter are in my opinion Italy's finest and, of course, I have added a couple of traditional English recipes with a Gino twist.

If you are on a diet you have two options: either choose the Bellini in Gelatina (page 143) or go for a ten-mile run and then choose whatever you want!

Cooking tips

1. There aren't any rules for desserts - you should have the ones you fancy
2. If you are having fish as a main course, the Torta al Limoncello (page 152) would be my recommendation as it will remove any fishy aftertaste
3. I think it is worth spending time making a really good dessert, as it is the one dish that your guests will remember
4. If you are making the Biscotti (page 154), make sure you serve a good-quality coffee with them
5. If you are having a lot of guests, the last thing you want to serve is Zabaglione (page 144) — too time consuming
6. If you want to impress, go for the Double Chocolate Mousse with Pistachio and Chilli (page 146)
7. Serve your desserts at least 20 minutes after the main course is finished
8. Forget cappuccinos and cafe lattes. After a big meal, the only thing to serve is an espresso, as milky coffee hinders digestion

Fresh Blackberry and Prosecco Jelly

Serves 6

130g caster sugar

Zest and juice of 1 unwaxed lemon

4 teaspoons powdered gelatine

50g strawberry purée

450ml Prosecco

180g blackberries

This has to be the most stylish and yet easy dessert that you will ever make. Not only can you use this dish as a dessert, but you can also serve it as a great aperitif. You can substitute the Prosecco for a good Champagne and if you don't want to use blackberries, you can use fresh strawberries. If you want to make fresh strawberry purée, just blitz 50g of fresh strawberries with 1 tablespoon of cold water and 1 teaspoon of honey into a smooth purée. Once the dessert is ready, you can decorate the jellies with a touch of whipped cream on top.

Put the sugar in a medium saucepan with 300ml of water and the lemon zest. Heat gently until the sugar has dissolved. Remove from the heat, leave to cool and discard the lemon zest.

Put the lemon juice in a small bowl and sprinkle in the powdered gelatine. Leave to soak for 3–4 minutes. Place the bowl over a pan of gently simmering water, ensuring that the base of the bowl does not touch the water, for a couple of minutes until the gelatine has completely dissolved.

Stir the gelatine into the sugar syrup together with the strawberry purée and the Prosecco. Mix well.

Meanwhile, share out three quarters of the blackberries among six Champagne glasses and carefully pour over enough of the liquid jelly to cover the fruit and chill until set. When the jelly has set, pour over the remaining liquid jelly to the top of the glass and refrigerate for 5 hours until completely set.

Decorate with the reserved blackberries and serve.

Zabaglione

Serves 4

5 really fresh egg yolks

120g caster sugar

8 tablespoons Marsala wine

4 tablespoons toasted hazelnuts, crushed

8 savoiardi biscuits (sponge fingers)

There is a rumour that zabaglione was used to give a man stamina before a night of passion. I don't believe everything I read but on this occasion, I can confirm that this is true.

Place the egg yolks, sugar and Marsala in a large heatproof bowl and set over a pan of simmering water, ensuring that the base of the bowl does not touch the water. (You also need to ensure that the bowl does not get too hot or the eggs will cook too fast and scramble.) Whisk continuously to achieve a smooth and foamy texture. When the mixture has tripled in volume, pour the hot zabaglione into four large wine glasses.

Decorate with crushed toasted hazelnuts on top and serve immediately with 1–2 savoiardi biscuits.

Tiramisu

Serves 4

300ml cold strong black coffee, preferably espresso

6 tablespoons Amaretto liqueur or a good Marsala wine

2 medium eggs, separated

3 tablespoons caster sugar

250g mascarpone cheese

250ml double cream, whipped

About 30 savoiardi biscuits (sponge fingers)

Cocoa powder, for dusting

Some people still believe that tiramisu is French in origin but that's rubbish. Tiramisu is the ultimate Italian dessert.

Pour the coffee into a large bowl, mix in 3 tablespoons of the Amaretto and set aside.

Beat the egg yolks and sugar in another large bowl for about 5 minutes until thick and pale. Add the mascarpone cheese and beat thoroughly to mix. Use a metal spoon to gently fold in the whipped cream.

Beat the egg whites in a third large bowl until soft peaks form. Fold them quickly, but gently, into the cream mixture, then add the remaining liqueur, trying not to lose the volume.

Dip each biscuit into the coffee for just 2 seconds and no longer, otherwise the biscuits will go soggy. Drain and use to cover the bottom of a glass dessert bowl about 8cm across (or four small ones). Spread some of the cream mixture over the biscuits, then repeat the process. Smooth the surface, cover with clingfilm and chill for about 2 hours to allow the flavours to develop. Just before serving (and not before or the cocoa powder will go bitter), remove the clingfilm and dust with cocoa powder.

Strawberry, Pistachio and Ricotta Soufflé

COPPETTE DI FRAGOLE

145

Serves 4

200g strawberries, sliced

3 tablespoons Amaretto liqueur

4 medium eggs, separated

130g caster sugar

325g ricotta cheese

1 tablespoon vanilla extract

30g pistachio nuts, finely chopped

Zest and juice of 1 unwaxed lemon

Butter, for greasing

Icing sugar, for dusting

This is the kind of dessert that will always put a smile on people's faces. I guess it must be because everybody thinks you put a lot of effort into making such a beautiful-looking and tasty dish. Well, let me tell you, it is definitely full of flavour, but it needs minimum effort to put it together. The only difficulty is that you need to be quite precise on the cooking time, so allow a good 30 minutes between the end of your main course and the beginning of your dessert. If strawberries are not in season, you can use any berries of your choice.

Preheat the oven to 180°C/350°F/gas mark 4. Place the strawberries in a small saucepan with the Amaretto and gently simmer for about 8 minutes until soft. Remove from the heat and leave to cool.

Beat together the egg yolks and the sugar in a large bowl until thick and pale. Add the ricotta, vanilla extract, pistachios, lemon zest and juice and mix thoroughly.

In a second large bowl, whisk the egg whites until stiff. Very gently fold into the ricotta mix.

Grease 4 ramekins and share out the strawberries and their juices between the dishes.

Spoon the ricotta mixture over the strawberries, level the tops, and bake in the centre of the oven for 30–35 minutes until puffed and lightly browned.

Dust with icing sugar and serve immediately.

SWEET THINGS

Double Chocolate Mousse with Pistachio and Chilli

MOUSE DI CIOCCOLATO CON PISTACCHIO E PEPERONCINO

Serves 4

150g good-quality dark chocolate, chopped

100g good-quality white chocolate, chopped

3 medium eggs, separated

2 tablespoons caster sugar

8 tablespoons pistachio nuts, crushed, reserving a few to decorate

1 small red chilli (medium–hot), deseeded and finely sliced

2 tablespoons Grand Marnier

250ml double cream, softly whipped

I think you will agree with me that nearly everybody likes chocolate mousse and if you are one of these people, you will absolutely love this recipe. I came across the combination of chilli and chocolate in Mexico, when I was filming my series 'An Italian in Mexico' and since then, I realised that the spiciness of the chilli with the sweetness of the chocolate is a match made in heaven. You can substitute the pistachio nuts for hazelnuts and please make sure that when you melt the chocolate, the glass bowl doesn't touch the simmering water, otherwise it will become bitter. Make sure you allow at least half an hour between the end of your main course and this fabulous dessert.

Melt all the chocolate together in a heatproof bowl over a pan of simmering water, ensuring that the base of the bowl does not touch the water. Set aside to cool, but not to harden.

Beat the egg yolks and sugar together in a large bowl until thick and pale.

Whisk the egg whites in a second large dry, clean bowl until stiff.

Use a metal spoon to fold the chocolate into the egg yolk mixture. Add the pistachios, chilli and Grand Marnier. Mix well and fold in the whipped cream. Lastly, gently fold in the egg whites, mixing the ingredients together.

Pour the mixture into four dessert glasses (each about 250ml), cover with clingfilm and chill for 3 hours until set.

Just before serving, remove the clingfilm and decorate with crushed pistachio nuts.

Panettone and Butter Pudding

Serves 4

800ml full-fat milk

Zest of 1 unwaxed lemon, finely grated

50g salted butter, at room temperature

6 slices Panettone, about 3cm thick

50g flaked almonds

3 medium eggs

45g caster sugar

3 tablespoons Cointreau

30g soft brown sugar

Icing sugar, for dusting

One of my favourite British recipes has to be a good bread and butter pudding. The simplicity of the flavours and the warm sensation it gives you is brilliant. I chose Panettone because after Christmas I always have too much left over and I wanted to create something else with it rather than just eat it with a cup of tea. The lightness of the Panettone is much better than normal bread and gives this dish a fantastic twist. My only tip for this recipe is to ensure that the Panettone is soaked into the milk mixture for at least 30 minutes, which will allow the pudding to grow in the oven like a soufflé.

Preheat the oven to 180°C/350°F/gas mark 4. Heat the milk with the lemon zest in a medium saucepan and bring to the boil. Remove from the heat and set aside.

Meanwhile, butter the Panettone and cut each slice into triangles.

Sprinkle half the almonds over the base of an ovenproof dish measuring about 25cm long and at least 8cm deep. Neatly overlap the Panettone over the almonds.

Beat together the eggs, sugar and Cointreau in a large bowl. Slowly add the milk and mix well. Spoon the mixture over the Panettone and leave to soak for about 30 minutes. Use your fingers to gently push the Panettone down into the mixture.

Sprinkle the top with brown sugar and place in a roasting tin. Pour in enough hot water to come halfway up the sides of the dish. Bake in the centre of the oven for 50–55 minutes until the custard is lightly set and the top is golden brown. Sprinkle the remaining almonds on top for the last 10 minutes of cooking.

Dust with icing sugar and serve immediately.

Fresh Fruit Pavlova

Serves 8

3 medium egg whites

180g caster sugar

1 teaspoon white wine vinegar

1 teaspoon cornflour

1 teaspoon vanilla extract

FOR THE FILLING

300ml double cream

2 kiwi fruit, peeled and sliced

100g strawberries, halved

3 passionfruit (cut in half and scoop out the pulp and seeds)

250g fresh pineapple, peeled, cored and cut into chunks

1 papaya, peeled, deseeded and sliced

3 tablespoons Limoncello liqueur

This is definitely one of those desserts that everybody should just tuck into and choose how much they want to eat. Simple to prepare and yet still has the wow factor. Every time I cook it for my friends or family, I hope to enjoy the leftovers with a cup of coffee in the morning, but I'm always disappointed as there is never any left. This dessert goes well after a long, heavy meal because of the fresh fruits and lightness of the meringue. My tip is to ensure that once you put the cream and the fruits into the meringue, you serve it within an hour, otherwise the meringue will start to get soggy in the middle.

Preheat the oven to 120°C/250°F/gas mark ½.

Whisk the egg whites in a large, clean, dry bowl until stiff. Whisk in the sugar a little at a time until stiff and very shiny. Whisk in the vinegar, the cornflour and the vanilla extract.

Draw a 20cm circle on a sheet of non-stick baking paper, and pour the meringue onto it, spreading it out to ensure that there is a substantial hollow in the centre.

Bake in the centre of the oven for 90 minutes or until light brown and dry. Press it gently with a finger to check that it is a little soft in the centre. Leave to cool on a rack, then peel away the baking paper.

In a large bowl, whisk the double cream until soft peaks form. In a separate bowl, mix together all the fruits with the Limoncello.

Spoon the whipped cream into the centre of the pavlova and top with the fruits.

Italian Chocolate and Nut Cake

Serves 4

250g good-quality dark chocolate

3 medium egg whites

50g candied peel

200g ground almonds

100g walnuts, crushed

50g hazelnuts, crushed

200g icing sugar

4 tablespoons Amaretto liqueur

FOR THE TOPPING

100g good-quality dark chocolate

70g icing sugar, plus extra for dusting

This is a traditional northern Italian recipe that comes from Siena. While I was at catering school, I came across hundreds of recipes on how to make a good Panforte and ten years ago, I decided that this would be the recipe that I was going to stick with. Historically, this dessert was used by the monks like a coin (hence the round shape), so they could trade for things they needed in the monastery. Please, please, please ensure that you use a good-quality dark chocolate, at least 70 per cent cocoa. This cake is also great for afternoon tea.

Melt the chocolate in a large heatproof bowl over a pan of simmering water, ensuring that the base of the bowl does not touch the water.

Use a fork to beat the egg whites in a large bowl for 2 minutes. Add in the peel, ground almonds, the nuts, icing sugar and Amaretto. Mix well, then very gently fold in the melted chocolate.

Line a circular flan dish measuring about 18cm across and 3cm deep with clingfilm. Pour in the mixture and set aside for 2 hours.

To make the topping, melt the chocolate in a heatproof bowl over a pan of simmering water, ensuring that the base of the bowl does not touch the water.

Melt the icing sugar and 2 tablespoons of water in a small saucepan over a low heat. Stir to check the sugar has melted, then add the chocolate to make a syrup.

Turn out the cake onto a plate and peel off the clingfilm. Use a spatula to cover the surface with the chocolate syrup. Set aside for 1 hour until the chocolate has hardened.

Serve in slices, dusted with icing sugar, with a cup of your favourite tea.

Limoncello and Plum Tart

TORTA AL LIMONCELLO

Serves 8

Zest and juice of 2 unwaxed lemons

4 tablespoons double cream

100g ground almonds

200g caster sugar

5 medium eggs

120g butter, melted

10 tablespoons Limoncello liqueur

6 plums, cut into wedges

Icing sugar, for dusting

FOR THE PASTRY

190g plain flour, plus extra for dusting

100g chilled unsalted butter, plus extra for greasing

This recipe comes from the beautiful town of Sorrento where Limoncello is used in nearly every dessert. In the south of Italy, we serve it after a big meal as a digestive served in a cold shot glass. If you don't fancy making the shortcrust pastry, feel free to use ready made – no one will know!

To make the pastry, sift the flour into a large bowl and use your fingertips to rub in the butter until the mixture resembles breadcrumbs. Add 2–3 tablespoons of cold water and mix to a dough. Bring together into a ball, wrap in clingfilm and chill for 20 minutes.

Roll out the pastry on a floured surface to fit a 25cm loose-based flan tin. Grease the tin with a little butter, then line it with the pastry. Leave to rest in the fridge for at least 2 hours.

Preheat the oven to 180°C/350°F/gas mark 4. Line the pastry with grease-proof paper, fill with baking beans and bake blind for 15 minutes. Remove from the oven and leave to cool before removing the beans and paper.

Put the lemon zest and juice in a large bowl. Add the cream, almonds, sugar, eggs and butter and mix together to a smooth paste using a hand blender. Stir in the Limoncello.

Arrange the plums on the base of the pastry case and pour the lemon mixture on top. Bake in the centre of the oven for 20 minutes. Turn off the oven and leave the tart to cool in the oven. To serve, decorate with a thick layer of icing sugar.

Apple and Pine Nut Cake
with Honeyed Mascarpone

Serves 6

100g raisins

5 tablespoons Marsala wine

5 tablespoons honey

250g mascarpone cheese

1.2kg Cox apples, peeled, cored, and cut into chunks

100g soft brown sugar

100g pine nuts

3 medium eggs

200g caster sugar

200g salted butter, at room temperature

200g ground almonds

5 tablespoons flaked almonds

There are three things that my mother-in-law gave me: number one her daughter, number two wisdom and love, and number three (most importantly) this recipe! I can't remember when, but one day she told me that she had an old recipe that was passed down from generations and she wanted to give it to me. Of course, being the good son-in-law I am, I tried it and absolutely loved it. Out of respect, I decided not to change anything about this dessert and am sure you will agree that it is fantastico.

Preheat the oven to 180°C/350°F/gas mark 4. Put the raisins in the Marsala and set aside to soak. Combine the honey and mascarpone in a small bowl, cover with clingfilm and chill until ready for serving.

Put the apples in a medium saucepan with the brown sugar and cook over a low heat until soft. Once ready, mix in the soaked raisins and pine nuts and set aside.

Cream the eggs and sugar in a large bowl. Add the butter and ground almonds and combine to give a smooth paste.

Place the apples in an oval baking dish measuring about 25cm long and 8cm deep. Spread the creamed mixture over the top.

Cook in the centre of the oven for about 30 minutes until golden brown. Sprinkle over the flaked almonds and cook for a further 10 minutes.

Serve hot, with a dollop of mascarpone cream on the side.

Italian-style Biscuits

BISCOTTI

Serves 4

2 whole medium eggs

3 medium egg yolks

150g caster sugar

300g plain flour, plus extra for dusting

100g hazelnuts, chopped

'Biscotti' means cooked twice, but I chose not to use the traditional method, because I found a way of simplifying the process while retaining a fantastic texture and flavour. The biscuits can be preserved in a sealed plastic container.

Preheat the oven to 160°C/325°F/gas mark 3 and line a baking tray with greaseproof paper.

Beat together the whole eggs and egg yolks in a large bowl. Use a wooden spoon to gently mix the sugar and the flour into the eggs. Add the hazelnuts and use your hands to fold in gently until you have a doughy mixture.

Turn out the dough onto a well-floured surface and roll into a sausage shape. Slice into diagonal strips each about 1.5cm thick.

Place the biscotti on the lined baking tray and bake for 17 minutes in the centre of the oven until golden. Turn out and cool on a rack until very firm.

Best with Italian coffee or vanilla ice cream.

Almond Biscuits

AMARETTI

Serves 4

Butter, for greasing

4 medium egg whites

350g caster sugar

350g ground almonds

30ml Amaretto liqueur

Preheat the oven to 180°C/350°F/gas mark 4 and line a baking tray with greaseproof paper. Lightly grease with the butter.

Whisk the egg whites in a large, clean, dry bowl until stiff and firm. Gently mix in the sugar and almonds. Pour in the Amaretto and fold in carefully to make a smooth paste.

Use a teaspoon to place small heaps of the mixture on the lined tray, spaced about 3cm apart to allow for expansion during cooking. Bake in the centre of the oven for about 15 minutes until golden brown.

Enjoy warm or dry the biscuits on a rack until crisp and firm.

Best served with coffee or ice cream.

Sometimes I find myself in situations where I can't quite find the words to express my feelings – and believe me for a man, that happens quite often.

I know that this is going to be the most popular chapter in the book, because I believe that the language of food is understood by everyone. Therefore, you have no more excuses not to tell your loved ones how you feel.

Cooking tips

1. This is the one instance when presentation is very important, so make an effort to ensure your food looks really fantastico

2. Make sure you have rehearsed this recipe at least once before so you won't feel too stressed on the night

3. A good bottle of wine or a cold glass of Champagne always goes down well

Sausage, Bean and Olive Casserole

SALSICCE E FAGIOLI

Serves 4

6 tablespoons olive oil

350g onions, chopped

2 carrots, chopped

400g pancetta, diced

1kg pork sausages, cut into chunks about 3cm thick

2 tablespoons plain flour

2 glasses red wine

80g tomato paste

400ml beef stock

150g pitted black olives

400g tinned cannellini beans, drained

200g button mushrooms, quartered

5 bay leaves

Salt and pepper

I always make this casserole for my best friend. A northern Italian classic, it is usually made with lard and pork belly, but I have updated it by replacing them with olive oil, sausages and pancetta. This way you get the strong flavour of the pork, but less cooking time. The combination of olives and pork is one that you will find in Italian restaurants now, and I love it. Try also replacing the sausages with small ribs. Leave the casserole to rest for about 10 minutes — you don't want to serve it scorching hot. It will be even better reheated the next day (just add a little water).

Preheat the oven to 200°C/400°F/gas mark 6. Heat the olive oil in a large flameproof casserole dish and fry the onions and carrots over a high heat for 2 minutes until golden.

Add in the pancetta and the sausages and cook for about 3 minutes, stirring with a wooden spoon. Mix in the flour and cook for a further minute, stirring continuously.

Add in the wine and cook for about 2 minutes to allow the alcohol to evaporate. Stir in the tomato paste, add in the beef stock, the olives, the cannellini beans and the mushrooms. Add the bay leaves, season with salt and pepper, and bring to the boil. Cover the pan and cook in the oven for 30 minutes until the sausages are tender and the sauce has thickened.

Serve with your favourite crusty bread.

'one for the boys'

Lamb Cutlets with Herb Crust and Warm Cannellini Bean and Fennel Salad

COSTOLETTE DI AGNELLO CON CROSTA

Serves 2

6 slices white bread

2 tablespoons finely chopped rosemary

2 tablespoons finely chopped sage

150g salted butter, melted

4 tablespoons olive oil

8 lamb cutlets

4 tablespoons Dijon mustard

FOR THE SALAD

300g tinned cannellini beans, drained

2 small fennel bulbs, thinly sliced

3 tablespoons extra virgin olive oil

1 tablespoon white wine vinegar

1 tablespoon chopped flat-leaf parsley

If I had to choose one meat, I would choose lamb – it's such a male meat with strong flavour. Served with a crust of sage and rosemary, the flavours are ten times better. I decided to serve my lamb cutlets with a warm fennel salad to give the dish a rustic look with plenty of colours and flavours. Of course, you can serve this dish with your favourite potatoes and use chops instead of cutlets. If the fennel is not in season, try French beans or pak choi.

Remove the crusts from the bread and blitz in a food-processor to form breadcrumbs. Place the crumbs in a large bowl and mix in the rosemary, sage and butter with your fingers. Season with salt and pepper and set aside. Preheat the oven to 200°C/400°F/gas mark 6.

Heat the olive oil in a large frying pan and seal the cutlets for 1 minute on each side to brown. (Work in batches, if necessary.) Transfer to a baking tray. Gently brush one side of the cutlets with the mustard and place 2 tablespoons of the breadcrumb mixture on top of each one.

Roast in the oven for about 10 minutes until the lamb is tender and the breadcrumbs are golden brown.

Meanwhile, place the beans and the fennel in a medium frying pan with 2 tablespoons of water. Cook over a high heat for about 5 minutes, stir in the extra virgin olive oil, the vinegar and the parsley. Season.

To serve, divide the warm salad between two plates and arrange four lamb cutlets around it.

Grind over some black pepper and serve immediately.

'for my husband'

Chicken in Marsala and Dill Sauce

Serves 2

2 skinless, boneless chicken breasts

Plain flour, for dusting

100ml olive oil

4 tablespoons Marsala wine

150ml double cream

1 tablespoon chopped dill

2 medium potatoes, unpeeled and par-boiled

2 garlic cloves, halved

2 tablespoons fresh rosemary, stripped from stalks

Salt and pepper

Every man at some point asks himself, 'what should I do to impress my girlfriend or wife?'. Of course, a diamond ring would be the first option, but for those who, like me, believe in 'minimum effort, maximum satisfaction', I would suggest that they get cooking. Trust me when I say that there is no woman on this planet who would not be seduced by this dish. The sweetness of the Marsala wine touching the cream and coating the chicken breast is amazing. Served with tasty sauté potatoes makes it perfect.

With a meat mallet, beat the chicken breasts between two sheets of clingfilm on a board until the breasts are 1cm thin. Lightly dust the breasts with flour.

Heat 2 tablespoons of the olive oil in a medium frying pan and fry the chicken for about 1 minute on each side. Add the Marsala and flame for about 15 seconds, allowing the alcohol to evaporate.

Add the cream and the dill, season with salt and pepper and cook, uncovered, over a low heat for about 4 minutes to allow the sauce to thicken.

Meanwhile, slice the potatoes about 1cm thick. Heat the remaining oil in a second frying pan, fry the garlic and rosemary for 1 minute, then add the potatoes. Season with salt and pepper and cook over a medium heat for 5 minutes or until golden on both sides.

Place a chicken breast on each plate and surround with sautéed potatoes. Drizzle some of the sauce over the chicken and serve immediately.

'for my beautiful wife'

Pasta with Lobster and Cherry Tomatoes

LINGUINE ALL'ARAGOSTA

Serves 2

1 whole live lobster (or a ready-cooked one, if you prefer)

4 tablespoons olive oil

1 garlic clove, finely sliced

1 small red chilli, deseeded and finely sliced

½ glass dry white wine

1 tablespoon freshly chopped flat-leaf parsley

10 cherry tomatoes, halved

250g linguine

Salt

I decided to write this recipe for one reason only: to prove to everybody that sometimes it's easier to cook a meal for someone than actually say 'I love you' to them. People need to be reminded how much somebody loves them and what better way to do so than this. I can understand that this recipe has an expensive ingredient, but don't worry, you can always replace it with large king prawns. Remember once the pasta is coated with the sauce, it needs to be served and eaten immediately, otherwise it will go dry and sticky.

Bring a large saucepan of water to the boil and cook the lobster for 10 minutes. Drain and leave to cool.

Twist off the claws and pincers. Using the back of a large, heavy knife, crack open the large claws. Use a skewer to carefully remove all the meat from the claws and cut into small chunks.

Place the lobster, back uppermost, on a flat surface and cut the lobster in half lengthways. Remove the meat from the body and cut into small chunks. Clean the shell under cold running water and set aside.

Heat the olive oil in a large frying pan and fry the garlic and the chilli for about 30 seconds over a medium heat, then add in the lobster meat and cook for about 1 minute. Add in the white wine, parsley, tomatoes, season with salt and continue to cook for about 5 minutes, uncovered, stirring occasionally.

Meanwhile, cook the pasta in a large pan of boiling salted water until al dente. Drain and add to the lobster sauce. Mix well over a low heat for 1 minute to allow the pasta to absorb the flavours of the lobster sauce.

To serve, spoon the pasta into the cleaned lobster shell, pour over any remaining sauce and enjoy immediately.

'I love you'

Duck Breasts in Limoncello Sauce

PETTO D'ANATRA AL LIMONCELLO

Serves 6

6 duck breast fillets (about 180g each)

4 tablespoons olive oil

Handful of fresh mint leaves, to garnish

FOR THE SAUCE

120g salted butter

2 tablespoons mixed peppercorns

200ml Limoncello

Zest and juice of 1 unwaxed lemon

300ml chicken stock

Salt and pepper

I have to admit that I don't often cook duck at home. One of the reasons is that I always save it for when I'm out in some friend's restaurant, but if I have to cook it, I would only use this recipe. The flavour of the Limoncello sauce works beautifully with duck breasts, and it doesn't take long to cook. Remember to rest the duck before slicing to allow the meat to relax. If you really don't fancy duck, you can use a good steak. Why for the girls? Because they love Limoncello.

Place the duck breasts in a large bowl and use your hands to rub in the olive oil with some salt and pepper.

Preheat the oven to 200°C/400°F/gas mark 6 and set a dry griddle pan to heat on the hob. Place the oiled breasts on the hot griddle, skin-side down first, and seal for about 2 minutes on each side. Transfer to a roasting tin and roast in the oven for about 10 minutes until it is crisp on the outside but pink in the middle. Remove from the oven and leave to rest for 1 minute before slicing each breast on the diagonal into four.

Meanwhile, prepare the sauce. Melt half the butter in a large frying pan, add the peppercorns and cook over a medium heat for 1 minute. Add in the Limoncello with the lemon zest and juice and simmer, uncovered, until reduced by half. Add the chicken stock, season with salt and pepper and continue to cook for about 8 minutes until the sauce is again reduced by half. Add the remaining butter to the sauce and stir with a wooden spoon until you create a creamy texture.

Place the sliced duck in the middle of a serving plate. Drizzle over the sauce, garnish with fresh mint leaves and serve immediately.

'something for the girls'

Chicken and Mediterranean Vegetable Pie

TORTA DI POLLO E VEGETALI

Serves 4

300g potatoes, peeled and cut into 2cm chunks

300g leeks, cut into 2cm chunks

2 carrots, peeled and cut into 2cm chunks

100g parsnips, cut into 1cm chunks

1 chicken stock cube

50g salted butter

1 garlic clove, chopped

3 skinless, boneless chicken breasts, cut into 2cm chunks

50g plain flour

100g Dolcelatte cheese

2 courgettes, finely sliced

2 tablespoons chopped fresh chives

1 medium egg, beaten

Salt and pepper

FOR THE PASTRY

300g plain flour, plus extra for dusting

120g salted butter, at room temperature

70g freshly grated Parmesan cheese

1 medium egg

I have never been a big fan of pies, but things changed when I came to live in England. I started to appreciate them so, of course, I've had to design one with my own signature.

To make the pastry, mix the flour with a pinch of salt in a large bowl and rub in the butter with your fingers to create a breadcrumb texture. Mix in the Parmesan and make a well in the centre. Add the egg and about 2 tablespoons of cold water. Knead until firm, wrap in clingfilm and chill in the fridge for about 30 minutes.

Cook the potatoes, leeks, carrots and parsnips in about 600ml of boiling salted water for 10 minutes until softened. Drain, reserving the liquid and mix with the stock cube and more water to give 600ml of stock.

Melt the butter in a saucepan and fry the garlic for about 30 seconds. Add the chicken and cook over a medium heat for about 3 minutes, stirring, until golden on all sides. Remove the pan from the heat and mix in the flour with a wooden spoon. Return the pan to the hob and continue to cook over a medium heat for about 2 minutes. Slowly add the stock, bring to the boil and cook for a further 3 minutes.

Add in the Dolcelatte, courgettes, the cooked vegetables, the chives, then season and stir well. Spoon the mixture into a 1.5-litre pie dish.

Preheat the oven to 180°C/350°F/gas mark 4. Roll out the pastry on a floured surface and mark out a round or oval shape to fit the top of your dish. Moisten the rim of the dish with water and place the pastry on top. Press the edges to seal and trim away any excess pastry. Garnish with some leaf shapes made from the pastry trimmings and brush beaten egg over the entire pie.

Bake in the centre of the oven for about 40 minutes or until the pastry crust is a lovely golden brown colour. Serve immediately.

'for my special family'

Sticky Banana and Chocolate Tart

BANANE AL CARAMELLO

Serves 6

50g salted butter

120g golden caster sugar

6 firm large bananas, peeled

100g chocolate chips

250g ready-to-roll puff pastry

Plain flour, for dusting

1 tub good-quality vanilla ice cream, to serve

What a fantastic way to end a meal. So far, I don't think I've met anyone, especially children, who doesn't like this recipe. I promise you that once you've made this dish and realise how easy it is to do, it will become a favourite. My tip would be to make sure that you bake the tart in the middle of a preheated oven to avoid the pastry burning. If you have to, you can replace the bananas for firm large pears, peeled and cut in half.

Melt the butter with the sugar in a deep-sided, heavy-based frying pan that can be used in the oven. Cook over a medium heat for about 5 minutes until it turns into golden caramel. Remove from the heat and set aside to cool slightly. Preheat the oven to 200°C/400°F/gas mark 6.

Place the whole bananas in the pan creating a circle, breaking as necessary, ensuring that the entire base is covered. Sprinkle over the chocolate chips.

Meanwhile, unroll the puff pastry onto a floured surface and cut a disc shape about 25cm diameter, or about 5cm bigger than the top of your pan.

Lay the pastry over the bananas and tuck the overlap down inside the pan with your fingers.

Bake the tart for 20–25 minutes or until the pastry is golden brown. Remove from the oven and set aside to cool for about 5 minutes.

Take a large circular plate and place face down on top of the pan. Quickly invert the pan to turn the tart upside down. Remove the pan, leaving the bananas facing upwards.

Serve generous portions with vanilla ice cream.

'for my children'

Chicken Breasts in Pizza Sauce with Mozzarella

POLLO ALLA PIZZAIOLA

Serves 4

8 tablespoons olive oil

3 garlic cloves, finely sliced

4 large skinless, boneless chicken breasts

800g tinned chopped tomatoes

1 teaspoon dried oregano

2 Mozzarella balls, drained and finely sliced

Salt and pepper

Being Neapolitan, it was easy for me to design a recipe with chicken and the same flavours as a pizza margherita. This is definitely a winner when you have your best friend over for dinner and is also very quick to prepare leaving plenty of time for chatting. My tip would be not to buy buffalo Mozzarella, because it contains too much water – just buy normal cow's milk Mozzarella. Make sure you have plenty of warm crusty bread to soak up the sauce.

Heat the olive oil in a large frying pan and fry the garlic and the chicken over a medium heat for 2 minutes on each side until golden.

Add in the tomatoes and oregano and season with salt and pepper. Cook, uncovered, over a medium heat for about 10 minutes until some of the water from the tomatoes has evaporated. Meanwhile, preheat the grill.

Remove the pan from the heat and place the sliced Mozzarella on top of the chicken breasts. Grind over some black pepper and place the pan under the grill for about 2 minutes or until the cheese starts to melt. (Protect the handle of the frying pan with foil, if necessary.)

To serve, pour some of the sauce in the middle of a each plate, place a breast of chicken on top and enjoy with warm crusty bread.

'for my best friend'

Saffron Risotto with Courgettes and Pork

RISOTTO ALLO ZAFFERANO

Serves 4

20g vegetable stock cube

5 tablespoons olive oil

1 onion, finely chopped

2 courgettes, cut into ½cm cubes

1 teaspoon finely chopped fresh
rosemary

200g minced pork

400g Arborio rice

½ teaspoon powdered saffron

200ml dry white wine

80g salted butter

100g freshly grated Parmesan
cheese

Salt and pepper

Saffron is a very popular ingredient in Italy especially in a risotto recipe. This dish comes from the northern part of Italy and is a classic to which I've added my own twist. A warm and comforting dish that will leave you truly satisfied. I never had the chance to cook this dish for my grandfather, but I'm sure he would have loved it.

Make up hot stock by dissolving the vegetable stock cube in 1.2 litres of boiling water. Pour into a jug and set aside.

Heat the olive oil in a large saucepan and fry the onion over a medium heat for about 2 minutes until softened. Add in the courgettes, rosemary and pork and keep cooking for a further 3 minutes, stirring continuously with a wooden spoon. Add the rice and keep stirring for 3 minutes, allowing the rice to toast in the olive oil and start to absorb all the flavours.

Add in the saffron, then the wine and continue to cook for a further 3 minutes to allow the alcohol to evaporate.

Start to add the warm stock a little at a time, season well and cook gently, stirring occasionally until the stock is absorbed. Continue adding more stock as each addition is absorbed. If necessary, add a little more hot water to the stock.

When most of the stock has been absorbed (about 20 minutes), taste the rice and make sure it is al dente. Remove the saucepan from the heat and add the butter to the risotto. At this point, it is very important that you stir the butter very fast into the rice for at least 1 minute – this creates a fantastic creamy texture.

Stir in the Parmesan and serve immediately.

'for my fantastic grandparents'

Chicken in Breadcrumbs with Tomato Salsa and Spicy Spinach

Serves 2

8 tablespoons olive oil

250g spinach leaves

1 garlic clove, sliced

½ teaspoon crushed dried chilli

2 large skinless, boneless chicken breasts

Plain flour, for dusting

2 medium eggs, seasoned and beaten

70g toasted fine breadcrumbs (see page 8)

Salt and pepper

FOR THE SALSA

3 large fresh plum tomatoes, chopped, seeds and skin included

2 tablespoons pitted black olives, sliced

5 fresh basil leaves, chopped

2 tablespoons extra virgin olive oil

I dedicate this recipe to all the dads for two reasons: firstly because my own father loves this dish, but also because this is my all-time favourite and I would love my boys to cook it for me one day. The combination of the crispy coated chicken with the spicy spinach is absolutely fantastic. Ensure that the topping for the chicken marinates for at least half an hour and try to get good-quality tomatoes. You can substitute chicken for veal or pork.

For the salsa, mix the tomatoes, olives and basil in a large bowl, drizzle with the extra virgin olive oil and season with salt and pepper. Mix well and allow to rest.

Heat 2 tablespoons of olive oil in a large frying pan and fry the spinach with the garlic and chilli. Season with salt and cook over a medium heat for about 4 minutes until softened. Keep stirring with a wooden spoon.

With a meat mallet, beat the chicken breasts between two sheets of clingfilm on a board until the breasts are 1cm thin. Lightly dust the breasts with flour, dip in the beaten eggs and finally coat in the breadcrumbs.

Heat the remaining olive oil in a large frying pan and gently fry the chicken over a medium heat for about 3 minutes on each side until golden and crisp. Transfer to kitchen paper to allow the excess oil to drain.

Place a chicken breast in the centre of each plate, spread 3 tablespoons of the tomato salsa on top and serve immediately with the spicy spinach.

'I love you, Daddy'

Conversion chart

WEIGHT (SOLIDS)	
7g	¼oz
10g	½oz
20g	¾oz
25g	1oz
40g	1½oz
50g	2oz
60g	2½oz
75g	3oz
100g	3½oz
110g	4oz (¼lb)
125g	4½oz
150g	5½oz
175g	6oz
200g	7oz
225g	8oz (½lb)
250g	9oz
275g	10oz
300g	10½oz
310g	11oz
325g	11½oz
350g	12oz (¾lb)
375g	13oz
400g	14oz
425g	15oz
450g	1lb
500g (½kg)	18oz
600g	1¼lb
700g	1½lb
750g	1lb 10oz
900g	2lb
1kg	2¼lb
1.1kg	2½lb
1.2kg	2lb 12oz
1.3kg	3lb
1.5kg	3lb 5oz
1.6kg	3½lb
1.8kg	4lb
2kg	4lb 8oz
2.25kg	5lb
2.5kg	5lb 8oz
3kg	6lb 8oz

VOLUME (LIQUIDS)	
5ml	1 teaspoon
10ml	1 dessertspoon
15ml	1 tablespoon or ½fl oz
30ml	1fl oz
40ml	1½fl oz
50ml	2fl oz
60ml	2½fl oz
75ml	3fl oz
100ml	3½fl oz
125ml	4fl oz
150ml	5fl oz (¼ pint)
160ml	5½fl oz
175ml	6fl oz
200ml	7fl oz
225ml	8fl oz
250ml (0.25 litre)	9fl oz
300ml	10fl oz (½ pint)
325ml	11fl oz
350ml	12fl oz
370ml	13fl oz
400ml	14fl oz
425ml	15fl oz (¾ pint)
450ml	16fl oz
500ml (0.5 litre)	18fl oz
550ml	19fl oz
600ml	20fl oz (1 pint)
700ml	1¼ pints
850ml	1½ pints
1 litre	1¾ pints
1.2 litres	2 pints
1.5 litres	2½ pints
1.8 litres	3 pints
2 litres	3½ pints

LENGTH	
5mm	¼ inch
1cm	½ inch
2cm	¾ inch
2.5cm	1 inch
3cm	1¼ inches
4cm	1½ inches
5cm	2 inches
7.5cm	3 inches
10cm	4 inches
15cm	6 inches
18cm	7 inches
20cm	8 inches
24cm	10 inches
28cm	11 inches
30cm	12 inches

Index

Acknowledgements

It would have been impossible to write this book without the help of my wife Jessie, who spent many nights translating my ideas and feelings onto paper. And of course, thank you to my two boys Luciano and Rocco, who spent many nights sleeping so I could actually write this book, Vi amo.

A big thank you to everybody at Kyle Cathie who made my dream come true. It's been a pleasure working with you – you made the ride easy and fun. Also thanks to Kate for the fantastic pictures, making me look half decent after many a late night.

A special grazie goes to everybody at Bontà Italia for the continuing support and understanding, Marco, you are the best!

A big kiss to Ali, who spent many days in the kitchen testing out my recipes, and to her family who were forced to eat them.

This is probably my only chance to really express my gratitude to my fellow colleagues who have supported and helped me in my television career: Jeni Barnett – I love you, Ainsley Harriott – a true friend, Antony Worrall Thompson – you are my wisdom and dictionary and finally, the guys at Prospect Pictures for giving me a chance. (Barry – my Pozzo di Scienza – auto-cue is now mastered).

Last, but not least, a huge thank you to the Don (ladies and gentlemen – Mr Jeremy Hicks) who continues to guide me in the right direction and believed in me from day one. You are not just my agent, you are someone I respect, admire and love like a father.

Grazie, grazie, grazie to all of you for choosing my book – Buon Appetito!

This edition published in 2012 by Kyle Books, an imprint of Kyle Cathie Ltd 192–198 Vauxhall Bridge Road London, SW1V 1DX general.enquiries@kylebooks.com www.kylebooks.com

First published in Great Britain in 2007 by Kyle Cathie Limited

10 9 8 7 6 5 4 3 2 1

ISBN: 978-0-85783-270-2

Gino D'Acampo is hereby identified as the author of this work in accordance with Section 77 of the Copyright, Designs and Patents Act 1988.

Editorial Director: Muna Reyal
Designer: Carl Hodson
Photographer: Kate Whitaker
Home economist: Annie Nichols
Styling: Penny Markham
Copyeditor: Stephanie Evans
Production: Sha Huxtable and Alice Holloway

A Cataloguing In Publication record for this title is available from the British Library.

Colour reproduction by Chromagraphic
Printed and bound in China by C&C Offset Printing Co., Ltd.